Acknowledgements

To mom and dad for starting me down this crazy path in life and pointing me in all the right directions. Your support in everything has made all the difference.

To Bill, Mike, Steve, Matt and all my friends who have been important parts of this journey. Our shared experiences of both happiness and misery (mostly misery) will always be special to me.

To Rachael for your unconditional love and for being a wonderful wife and mother. You have given me the greatest gift in my life.

To Nolan, I apologize in advance for exposing you to this madness. But it is my greatest wish to share as many happy memories with you as possible. I hope you have better luck than I have, and you're off to a good start.

And to the Flyers, in advance, on the off-chance that one day they'll give me something in return.

*

Contents

*

A Note from the Author

Whenever you undertake a project like this book, one that involves an ongoing storyline that has the potential to change at any given time, you take a risk. As I began writing in the spring of 2017, I chose to approach the topic of Philadelphia sports fandom from a specific angle and wanted to make a point about how special it is despite the general lack of ultimate reward for the fan base as a whole and for me personally. Do you see where I'm going with this? Most of my work was complete, and then the Eagles happened.

As their season rolled along, I started to slow down in my writing as I waited to see how things would turn out for them, fully expecting another painful addition to this book's catalog of disappointments. But they were not to be denied. Rewriting the textbook definition of the word "team", the 2017 Eagles took us to sports heaven and made so many of the setbacks of years past wash away in an instant. Did this championship put a dent in some of what I had already written? Yes. But it in no way undermines the overall spirit of the book. Somebody still had to tell the tale of the last few decades of Philadelphia sports and speak for the generation of fans that has lived through and dealt with it.

The aim of my writing isn't for all of us to simply dwell on losses or bemoan that our teams never win. Yes, some of that happens, but all of the events and accounts herein are meant to demonstrate one immutable fact: Philadelphia's fans are the most passionate, loyal and resilient ones around. And if you don't agree, you can stop reading right now. Many of you are just as fanatical as I am, and so this is your story, too.

For more occasions than we would like to admit, it has been a struggle as we have stood by our teams. Yes, high points have come and gone, and I make sure to detail those just as much as the tough times. By and large, however, we have gotten used to that ever-present feeling of dread deep within ourselves. But no more. Like my favorite film, *The Shawshank Redemption*, we are all Andy Dufresne, crawling through a river of excrement and coming out clean on the other side. It appears that years of suffering have led to a new beginning for us, and it feels so good.

So please enjoy as I attempt to put into words our shared ups and downs as Philadelphia fans over the past quarter-century and incorporate personal anecdotes and experiences for even more flavor and perspective that will be new to you. Spoiler alert: There's a happy ending.

Welcome to Zihuatenajo.

*

I'M GETTING A SPORTS COMPLEX

Trials & Tribulations
of a Thirtysomething Philadelphia Sports
Fan

See you around the sports complex!

Kevin Laspoli

This page intentionally left blank. So there.

1.
IN THE BIG INNING

I lied. I lied to you right in the title of this book. I'm not a Philadelphia sports fan. Yes, I do have the frequently sad distinction of liking its teams, but I was born and bred in the great state of Delaware. You know, that landmass dangling precipitously from the Keystone State's southeast corner. And so for the purposes of this exercise, my being a "Philadelphia fan" refers to my rooting interests, not my physical location. So, I'm not a Philadelphian, or even a native Pennsylvanian, but close enough. Let's move on.

People from some parts of the "Ware-House" as I have heard it called (solely by one delusional person that I work with) may be geographically closer to Baltimore/DC and root for teams from those areas, but up here in the north "above the canal" people largely bleed Eagles green, Flyers orange, and Phillies red, although that might just be regular blood from all of the shootings in Wilmington. Murdertown USA, baby.

Truthfully, it's an easy trip up and down I-95 to get to and from Philly. Delaware fans have it much easier than people from Philly's own suburbs who have to fight that horrible infrastructure and gridlock to make it to the sports complex. And we have it WAY WAY easier than fans from South Jersey who need to cross a bridge both ways, pay a toll, and also live in New Jersey. Ew. Throw in tax-free shopping and really low property taxes, and Delaware is the place to be. Paid for by the Delaware Tourism Board. We have like three state parks.

As best as I can piece together (and I really should nail this down before too many of my family members pass away), my great grandparents on my father's side came over from "the old country" and settled in Philadelphia early in the 20th century. I'm not sure if any love of sport existed there or if they were too busy just trying to get two nickels to rub together, but I do know that my grandfather (born 1915) was a very big fan. And so it began.

I can only assume that given the choice between the Phillies and Athletics, my grandfather preferred rooting for and going to see the A's because they were actually good. But with teams from both leagues in town, he took advantage of that to see every team in baseball in any given year. I remember hearing stories about him seeing Babe Ruth play at Shibe Park. Man,

I wish I had some of those ticket stubs today. Or maybe he just got the ticket sent to his phone when he bought them and they scanned the barcode. In that case, I'd have been out of luck.

Years later, my newly married grandparents left Philadelphia for the "suburbs" of Delaware. This turned out to be a good move because I wouldn't exist if they didn't. Seventy-some years later, their decision to relocate still reverberates. I like living here and what the area has to offer. So unless someone wants to blow me away with a job offer elsewhere, I'm probably not going anywhere anytime soon.

Time rolled on and by the mid-50's when my dad arrived in the world, it was just the Phillies left playing baseball in town. My father was a little kid when the epic collapse of 1964 occurred. To his credit, he didn't immediately jump out of his bedroom window upon realizing how unfulfilling his sports fandom would be for pretty much his entire life. But I'm sure that it really really sucked. Anyway, I didn't exist yet, so that'll be the last mention of that '64 season in this book.

From what I gather in talking to him, my dad spread his interests among all the teams in town. But the real game changer came when the NHL decided to expand into Philadelphia. The Flyers came into being in 1967. I'm not sure if my dad, his friends, and other young people in the area caught on initially or were simply wondering what the hell was going on with this strange sport. But within about five years, apparently the whole Delaware Valley was talking about it, with kids playing street hockey and dodging cars all throughout the tri-state area. The excitement was building, and so were the Flyers. (I stole that line from the 1988 team video).

Anyone with half a pulse knows what came next. Titles! Back to back Stanley Cups for the Flyers in 1974 and 1975 cemented their place for eternity in the city and its surrounding area. And, most importantly, in the hearts and minds of that generation of fans. When I see the videos and hear the stories about these teams some 40+ years later, I have mixed emotions which have evolved within me as I have gotten older. Awe, happiness, inspiration, excitement…a lot of it can still get me pumped up for a season or big game even today. But after several decades of following this team, even though I love them with every ounce of bone marrow I have, hearing old-timers recalling and dwelling on "the good old days" mostly leaves me frustrated and angry.

Where the hell is my Stanley Cup?

I would step in front of a bus to see this damn team win a championship. I already got too old to truly "share" one with my dad but I will still gladly take my first one now, with him in his 60's and me in my 30's. He doesn't say anything about it, but I'm sure he feels robbed too. In his case, when a team wins two titles before you turn 21, you probably expect a lot more and have to feel a little bit hollow when you're reaching retirement age and have yet to add another. And so decades of frustration build and build, trickling down to future generations.

Philadelphia would notch a couple other titles between those Flyers' Cups and the time that I was born. The 1980 Phillies must have been the best feeling in the world for my dad. They were so bad and painful to watch for years before they finally put it all together and climbed the mountain. Hearing about this all throughout my childhood, adolescence, and young adulthood filled me with the same kinds of feelings as the Flyers' stuff that I mentioned, but with the notable exception that it actually had a payoff in 2008 and doesn't still insufferably continue in the same case of championship blues that the Flyers have saddled with me with to this day.

The other title was the 76ers in 1983. I guess it was a big deal, but since my family has never been huge on basketball, it's not a subject that I have ever explored with my dad or others who were around for it. All the same, it was nice for the town to make another notch in its title belt. As all this was going on, I guess my dad's life began to include other pursuits and he got married. I don't believe my mom really followed sports very much at that point but I'm sure she was extremely excited for my dad when the Phillies won. She would also dutifully go to a bunch of his baseball games, giving the kind of support that we can all only hope for from someone we love. I like to picture her getting really into the games and swearing at the umpires. I would have paid to see that. And so my mom was also pulled into my family's sports vortex. She was quite the bowler too.

Skip ahead to 1984 and I was born. Strangely, I don't recall this happening or even being a baby. I mean, my parents tell all these stories, but how do I know what's true? I'm sure I just wallowed in my own crap until high school. I can't say that I remember specifically when I attended my first Phillies game at Veterans Stadium. Big fail on dad's part not posting a bunch of pictures on Facebook to commemorate it. But whenever it was, I'm sure it was also the first time I saw someone pissing in a bathroom sink.

My first Flyers game, I can tell you, was a Saturday afternoon game against the Blackhawks. The Flyers were a middling team at that point, missing the playoffs several years in a row, but they beat a pretty good Chicago team that day. I probably also saw someone pissing in the sink of the Spectrum that day, but I blocked it out if I did.

And how about those bathrooms at the Spectrum? You had to go down a flight of stairs to get to them. If your seats were upstairs it was like a 15-minute round trip if there was any foot traffic. And some days the distinct smell of the nearby refineries permeated the room. Well, it was either that or the B.O. from the Rangers' fans in attendance.

As for pre- and post-game urination, the receptacle of choice was usually the dilapidated shell of old JFK Stadium, which sat where the Wells Fargo Center is now. I can remember drinking a soda in the car on the way there and not thinking I could make the long walk to the Spectrum as we pulled into the lot. "Just use that", my dad said, pointing at JFK. After the game, we'd never want to get stuck in the mass of humanity at the downstairs bathroom so, again, JFK received my stream. Man, what an eyesore that thing was. The city just let it go sometime after Live Aid, and it crumbled away before being torn down in the mid-90's to make way for the new building.

From the time we parked to the time we walked through the Spectrum's turnstiles, we'd almost always stop to grab some pretzels to take inside. Boy, did I cut my gums on so many of those "soft" pretzels. "Three for a dolla". I'm not sure if outside food, if you can call those things food, were expressly prohibited by the airtight security, but it was probably a "just keep it out of sight" policy. So my dad would always hand the paper bag-o-pretzels to me for smuggling in. Nobody would ever suspect the round bespectacled kid in the Starter jacket. Mwahahahaha. And truly, there was nothing as sweet as the fine particles of the brown paper bag adhering to the salt and sinking into the pretzels. High in fiber no doubt.

One of the people I associate most vividly with the Spectrum, and no discussion of this edifice would be complete without me mentioning him, wasn't a player or a coach or an announcer. It was a vendor. I have no idea what the guy's name is but I have seen him at various sports events in Philadelphia and even some Orioles games in Baltimore over a span of 20+ years.

He was a droopy-faced short guy that would dutifully roam the stands hocking the normal sporting event fare. One day in particular, as he slowly ascended the stairs near us with a tray of chocolate-dipped vanilla cones, his voice rang out "Ice cream! Ice cream!" What also rang out was about half a lung as he was absolutely hacking all over them. Some poor guy somewhere probably wonders where the mixed nuts on his cone came from that day. Hence, the "Ice Cream Man" was born. He lives forever in the hearts and minds of Philadelphia fans, is a charter member of the Stadium Vendor Hall of Fame and, per my friend Frank's suggestion, really makes me want to write a coffee table book of stadium vendors. I think it would be a must-read for real fans.

But still, the Spectrum was awesome. It was great spending my formative years as a hockey fan in that cramped, dingy old barn. It's also funny how a sports arena not yet 30 years old can come across as this, meanwhile my house is 60+ years old and I think it's fine. Lending this some credence, though, I do feel pretty broken down some days in my 30s now.

Years after attending my last Flyers game at the Spectrum, I was truly taken back in time when I ventured up to Nassau Coliseum for a Flyers-Islanders game during the Isles' final season playing there in 2015. The layout was similar to that of the Spectrum. It was old and tight but had great sightlines for the game. The kicker was that it had that same stale popcorn (I hope it was popcorn) smell that I remember so vividly assaulting my olfactory senses at the Spectrum. I loved it. Of course, the Flyers got their heads kicked in that day. So much for memory lane.

The Spectrum would also prove to be the site of the single greatest sporting event I have ever witnessed and am likely to see in person for my entire life: March 28, 1992. Duke-Kentucky NCAA East Regional Final. Do I even need to go into detail with this one? I'm sure you can picture Christian Laettner catching the inbounds heave from Grant Hill, dribbling and putting up "The Shot". You know it was a pretty special moment and game when the final play from it is commonly referred to as THE SHOT.

So yeah, I was there, and I have no idea why. I think my dad's friend couldn't make the game so he took me with him. I remember being mildly interested in college basketball then and knew who the good teams were. But to go to a game of that magnitude to begin with, let alone what ended up happening, was pretty damn special. Obviously I didn't appreciate it at the time, but I do remember someone saying as we were leaving that "That was the greatest game of all-time". Hyperbole? Maybe. But it makes all the lists, so who am I to argue with the "experts"?

On the other side of the coin, basketball is well down my list of favorite sports, so for this to be the biggest event I've ever attended is a bit soul-crushing. It didn't even involve a team that I care about. Over a quarter-century later, I have resigned myself to this being the high water mark of events I'll ever attend. Unless I somehow get my hands on Game 7 World Series tickets and the Phillies win it in the bottom of the 15th inning on a grand slam by Chase Utley Jr., Duke-UK is it. 7-year old me would have been extremely upset if he knew this at the time. Even now, it bums me out to some degree.

Just one year later, however, something much more important to me occurred. It was the magical 1993 Phillies season. I'm sure I attended some games that year and could validate it by digging out some old stubs. But of course it's the playoffs that stick out in my mind. I was so jacked up to go to Game 2 of the NLCS, just days before my 9th birthday. The Phillies had won Game 1 against the hated Braves the night before in a thrilling 10-inning affair, the winning hit coming off the bat of all-time legend Kim Batiste. But there would no such magic with me in attendance for Game 2. The Braves won 14-3. They hit four home runs, the only one of which I remember was a ball that Fred McGriff put into orbit way over our heads in right field. The series was only 1-1 at that point, but I was upset. The first professional playoff game I had ever attended and it turned out like that.

The Phillies, however, would end up taking the series, clinching and setting the city into a frenzy while I was asleep on a school night. Playoff games started too damn late even back then. I'm kind of disappointed in myself that I didn't put up more of a fight to stay up and watch, but I guess school was kind of important. So it was onto the World Series for the first time in my life, as "Whoomp! There It Is" blared on a continuous loop throughout the area. Ridiculously enough, there is actually some confusion as to whether or not this was the song that people were singing or if it was "Whoot, There It Is" (two different songs by two different bands). But it was fun at the time, so who cares?

Those in my age group may remember specifics about the Series, but for me it's really a blur. All I know is that the Phillies dropped three of the first four and had their backs against the wall with Curt Schilling heading to the mound for Game 5. And my dad just so happened to have tickets. So I got to go to my first ever World Series game. I'm also going to presume that it will be the only one I'll ever attend because I'd be really hard-pressed to fork over the kind of money it would take to go nowadays. Oh yeah, and the Phillies would have to be good again.

Anyway, the Phillies scraped across two early runs in the game and that was more than enough for Schilling, who threw a five-hit shutout and showed himself to be a big-game pitcher, something he'd prove over and over again throughout his career with teams who would actually go on to win. I was over the moon about that one. I didn't focus on the fact that the Phillies would need to take two games in Toronto to pull off the comeback. Instead I enjoyed the moment and it was a true thrill to be in a Vet packed to the gills when I was so used to seeing it about 80% empty for April games against the Padres. And despite the futility of Philadelphia fandom that I was still in the early stages of, I was confident that they would win that night. Not once did it occur to me that a loss meant the Blue Jays celebrating and the trophy coming out at the end of the game. In retrospect it might have been cool to see because I doubt I'll ever be at a championship-clinching game. And it would have actually been preferable to what came next.

Joe Carter. Mitch Williams. That's all I have to say. If you don't know what happened, I don't know why you're reading this. Somewhat mercifully, I was asleep again (what the hell was wrong with me?) when it occurred. It was a Saturday night! I am still simultaneously annoyed and relieved that I didn't stay up. I was able to piece together what happened the next morning when I came downstairs, saw the newspaper (remember those?) and the look of total dejection on my father's face as he inattentively burnt the hell out of some pancakes.

Yeah, so 1993 really sucked. The only specific events I can recall are my grandfather dying, the Phillies losing the World Series, and then my other grandfather dying. I'm not saying those things are commensurate, but still, it would have been nice to not have a devastating loss hanging over the fanbase like that. The team's run was fun while it lasted though, really amazing when you think about it since they came out of nowhere. But little did we all know how long it would take the team to be that relevant and exciting again. The Schilling game ended up being the last Phillies playoff game at the Vet.

But I do have the '93 team to thank for giving me a guidepost back to which I can trace my fandom. Sure, I had been to a good deal of Phillies and Flyers games before that, as well as some other assorted sporting events. But that touchstone season and the near-miss that it encompassed really started me down my insane path. I was going to put everything I had behind these damn teams in the hope of getting a title or two or ten out of them.

*

2.

IT'S ALL FUN & GAMES UNTIL YOUR TEAMS SUCK

As a kid, I saw everything through sport goggles. Sometimes literally, as I briefly wore them playing baseball, decided they were stupid, and just wore my glasses from that point on. It was nice when I finally got contacts. But, in the more metaphorical sense I was going for, I was always playing sports, reading about them, thinking about them and was generally obsessed. When I was ten years old and we got a beagle, I named him Bernie in honor of Flyers goaltender Bernie Parent, who ranks as my favorite athlete that I never actually saw play in person. Bernie for life.

I would be genuinely upset if a family outing or something else got in the way and I had to miss a game. If a TV was nearby, I would be drawn to it. Embarrassingly, this behavior wasn't confined to early childhood and adolescence, as it continued much later into my life. Ok, fine, I still do this today. Just let me watch the game and don't bother me with other "obligations" and "things to do" and "funerals" that prevent me from seeing it.

The truth of the matter is that most of these individual games had very little bearing on anything. But in my childhood, every game felt like life and death to me. If the Flyers lost a game in January to Calgary, I was pissed and it ruined my mood basically until the next game. I appreciate that my parents just let me be and didn't try to show me the error of my ways. They figured I would grow out of it. They were right, of course. Mostly.

Kids overreact and get emotional about things like sports all the time. Nowadays I take the regular losses and other disappointments in stride, as a lifetime of emotional beatdowns and the proverbial death of hope within my soul have taught me to not get too bent out of shape after every game. I do, however, think it is vital for the sanity of the Philadelphia fan to pick and choose their spots to go absolutely ballistic.

Our investments of time, emotions and (frequently the most important of all) money entitle us to an effort and an end result that gives us great pleasure. And since the financial aspect of being a sports fan wasn't really part of the landscape when I was young, I was all-in on the emotional aspect. This meant frequently throwing things, slamming doors and getting all worked up after certain losses or even failures within games. I guess I felt like I had the right to treat other people like crap just because the Flyers got shut out or Chris Boniol missed a field goal (which happened a lot).

If the team was actually good enough to make the playoffs, when the inevitable elimination came that particular year, you did not want to be around me. I hope I wasn't the only kid who was this terrible. Obviously I've gotten better as I gain wisdom, experience and gray hair but it's still rough to think about. Weren't sports supposed to be fun? Suffering along with my teams really didn't feel like it a lot of the time. But luckily I could still play in games of my own that gave me an outlet to achieve some kind of success on my own rather than attempting to do so vicariously through the sad sack local teams. I played organized sports throughout my youth, but oftentimes games with friends were just as fun.

I have to imagine that youngsters in other parts of the country where teams were actually good approached their childhood sandlot ballgames differently than me and my friends did. If kids are fortunate enough to have a patch of grass to play on or a clear enough street for some stickball, you know they'll be emulating players from their favorite teams. And they almost assuredly would do it in a genuine way because they loved those players and the teams they suited up for. Said players were also probably good, maybe even to the point of having delivered a championship or two recently that these kids could revel in and relive on their neighborhood fields and streets.

But from my point of view, there were no sports heroes at that point. Just "that year's Eagles" or the "same old Phillies" that my friends and I could sarcastically adopt the form of and impersonate for our silly childhood games. From an early age, our group saw that the crop of athletes playing for our Philadelphia teams was largely a parade of clowns and nobodies. And we still find ourselves endlessly amused today at the mere mention of some players from the mid-to-late 90's. This probably makes up about 75% of the humor between me and my longest-tenured friends actually. And you always score bonus points for more obscure references.

For instance, just saying "John Kruk has one nut" only registers about a 7 out of 10 on our laugh-o-meter. (Yes, that's still funny to us). But if you simply say the name of someone who really sucked and/or was here for a brief time, you go off the charts. MIDRE CUMMINGS! See, there. You have to actually get the reference, but if you do, then you're rolling in the aisles.

That's literally all we do with some of these guys. Still! Today! We just say their names (sometimes with a special emphasis for added effect) or text them to each other. And my apologies to John Kruk, who was actually good. But when we associate something specific with a player, we never let it go. Case in point, Tony Barron barely played for the Phillies but made one of the greatest catches you'll ever see, an all-out dive and full body plant onto the turf at the Vet. It helps that I was at the game to spread his legend. Thus we always reference him and that catch. So on rare occasions, I guess it can actually work to a guy's benefit.

The games of sandlot or street baseball with my friends, and sometimes even dart baseball when we weren't able to get out and play, were made more fun by us "becoming" the actual players. This meant deciding on what teams we would be that day and then ACTUALLY HAVING TO CONSULT THE PHYSICAL BOX SCORE IN THE PAPER to see what their lineups looked like the previous day. We knew all the top players around the league obviously, but in order to get it as "realistic" as possible we had to see what their actual batting order looked like. With any luck, they used a lot of pinch hitters and relief pitchers the previous night, giving us more players in our arsenal for our re-creation.

We definitely had an inferiority complex from an early age, my friends and I, as we openly acknowledged how bad our teams were and basically just assumed they would never win anything. Even as kids, we knew that we were watching something terrible when guys like Desi Relaford and Ricky Otero weren't just there to fill out the squad, but were playing prominent roles on an everyday basis. When you see my list of disliked athletes later on in the book, it shouldn't come as any surprise how many of these types of guys appear on it.

Years later, on a whim I wrote a parody song set to the tune of Billy Joel's "We Didn't Start the Fire" called "Why Do We Like the Phillies?" It was a loving but condescending ballad that encompassed about a decade of terrible baseball. I don't have those lyrics anymore but the one line that stands out in my head and that was probably my favorite in the whole song was "Kevin Sefcik, David Doster, every year an awful roster". This was the kind of drek we were dealing with as kids. It's a wonder we still followed these teams.

On the Eagles front, as Rich Kotite's tenure thankfully gave way to the Ray Rhodes era, things seemed to be getting better. Those Eagles teams showed some life in the mid-90's but things were over seemingly as quickly as they begin, with Rhodes also getting the boot after four years at the helm.

I have a few main recollections from Ray Rhodes' tenure. First, the Eagles demolished the Lions in the 1995 playoffs but then got embarrassed by the Cowboys the following week. I still felt good about the direction of the team going into the next season, but they posted an identical 10-6 record from the previous year and seemingly took a step back after being shut out in the first round of the playoffs by the 49ers.

1997 brought renewed hope in the form of Bobby Hoying, who burst onto the Philadelphia sports scene like few ever have. But he turned out to be the ultimate flash in the pan. All across the Delaware Valley, there are probably still thousands of old Bobby Hoying shirts being employed as rags for washing cars and other such uses. I know my friend Bill got his jersey, probably for Christmas. I was jealous for about a week. The team bottomed out in 1998, going 3-13. Then it was time for Andy Reid and Donovan McNabb, which actually turned out to be fun and productive for a good long time.

I played my share of touch (and sometimes tackle) football games amongst friends, but probably the biggest football-related thrill that Bill and I ever got was being able to toss the pigskin around on the Veterans Stadium field with our dads. For a few years in the 90's, the Phillies held their "holiday phan phair" in December as a reward for their loyal season ticket holders like my dad, who had a partial plan. Being December, the field at the Vet was of course set up for football. And you were actually allowed down on the field one year so we took full advantage, rolling around on the painted concrete that was the Vet turf. I think those few minutes took about ten years of life out of my knees, so I can only imagine what the players went through.

In subsequent years, I remember the field being roped off and only the sideline made available for any playing. God forbid we traipse across the precious endzone and its "Navy" lettering from the Army-Navy game that had just been played there. It was always pretty funny to see that it was still visible as Bobby Abreu settled under fly balls in right field four months later. Way to go, grounds crew.

One year, while waiting for the gates to open, Bill and I had a catch underneath one of the big, ugly ramps that surrounded the Vet and which you had to ascend in order to reach the main entrance. One of Bill's throws got past me and the football managed to bounce up the angled support of the ramp and settle on a small flat area at the top. I made the climb to get it and didn't think anything of the pile of refuse at the top.

But as I prepared to come back down with the ball, a very low "Whatcha doing, man?" emanated from the human apparently swaddled in that lump of blankets and whatever else was there. Quite startled, I got out of there. I told Bill, and we both decided that I had just had an encounter with recently released backup catcher Lenny Webster. Hence, "Lenny" was born and lives on forever in our infantile rolodex of humor.

The highlight of the phan phair was the Phanatic dressing as Santa Claus, but other members of the Phillies' organization were also there and would meet and greet the fans. Immediately upon entering one year, we were received by team president Bill Giles and new managerial hire Terry Francona. I shook Mr. Giles' hand as he welcomed us, but I never did get a handshake from Francona. I don't recall why this was the case, but for whatever reason, I took it personally and just didn't like the guy from the start. My feelings would prove to be validated as he bungled his way through four bad seasons as the team's skipper. Admittedly, he was given next to nothing to work with, but anyone who thinks he was even adequate is kidding themselves.

This is why it positively boggles my mind that this man ever got another major league managing job, let alone go on to win multiple World Series. But that's just the way it typically goes in Philadelphia over and over again. Someone is terribly overmatched and falls woefully short of expectations here but then manages to thrive when they go to a different environment in a different city. Has it ever worked the other way around? Just once, I'd like to see one of our teams take on some kind of reclamation project and see him just go off the charts here. But I know this will never happen.

It was around this time period that I stopped going to games exclusively with my dad and would sometimes attend with a friend or two. On several occasions, I went with my friend Mike, his brother and their dad, who would bring a jug into the Vet with him which he had filled with several beers. All he had to tell the crack security staff was that it was iced tea and he was cheerily allowed to enter. Things were very different pre-9/11.

I also remember intricately studying how the seats at the Vet were bolted into the concrete on the off chance that I ever got to attend the last game there when it was time for the Phillies to move. I could bring the requisite tools with me to pull out some seats. In my mind, this would be the same as my dad and grandfather ripping out the old wooden seats at Connie Mack Stadium after its final game in 1970. But still, what the hell was I thinking? Needless to say, this plan never came to fruition, although my dad did end up buying a pair of seats later on, one of which was the end seat from the row so it has the Liberty Bell logo on it. This was another "perk" of having a ticket plan at the time.

At one particular Phillies-Braves game that I attended with Mike and his family, a torrential storm struck late in the game. While we ran for cover on the concourse, most fans left. I'm really surprised that we stayed as late as we did, but it wasn't a school night, so we stuck it out. After a lengthy rain delay, there were maybe 100 people left in the stands, so we slid down right behind the first base dugout.

With the Phillies trailing, hated Braves' reliever John Rocker entered the game. Mike and I had been at the stadium for about six hours at that point, but it didn't stop us from screaming "Rocker!" over and over again at the top of our lungs. I don't know how we weren't able to shake his confidence, but he nailed down the save. This was also one of several times that we got a thrill in the car ride on the way home as his dad called into WIP to make his normal complaints about Francona, Chris Wheeler, and probably some baserunning error that Bake McBride made in 1978.

I wasn't keeping good track of wins and losses at that point in time but was just trying to enjoy myself as much as possible while accepting that it probably wasn't going to end well. At one point, however, I did begin to buy scorecards and diligently kept score for the games I attended. I'm pretty sure I was the only teenage kid doing this anywhere. Looking back, I don't know how I had the patience and attention span to do this.

I would leave my seat maybe one time for a quick bathroom break or to get something to eat, handing the scorecard to my dad in case I missed anything while always being suspicious of whether or not he was up to the task. My far-reaching idea was that many years later I could look back on these games that I went to and have unassailable proof of all the Hall of Famers and other superb players that I got to see in person. I wanted something tangible, and so I kept score at every Phillies game I attended for a good six- or eight-year period. I did the same for many Orioles games, as well as at five or six other major league ballparks.

On my first visit to Shea Stadium to see the Phillies take on the Mets, a pitcher entered the game for New York who was not in the program, nor did they actually display his name on their old outdated scoreboard. And the public address announcement was so muffled I couldn't make heads or tails of it. After getting home from the game, I actually had to ask my friend on the phone who pitched the 7th inning for the Mets in the game I had just attended. This is absolutely ridiculous to think about now. Just like watching old episodes of *Seinfeld* where half of the storylines could be resolved immediately by people having cell phones, it was a different time and you just have to accept it for what it was.

In 1996, the MLB All-Star Game came to town and I was so excited about having a chance to go. We would also get to attend the undeniable highlight of the festivities, the home run derby. At that point in time, the derby took place in the afternoon on the day before the game and then was SHOWN ON TAPE DELAY THAT NIGHT. Are you kidding me?

We were sitting down the right field line, and I flailed my arm intentionally when Brady Anderson pulled a foul ball close to our section. Because of this, I was able to identify myself when watching the derby as it aired that night. What a thrill, my first national TV appearance. I had been at Camden Yards in Baltimore some years earlier when they filmed crowd scenes for *Major League II* but must have ended up on the cutting room floor. To get the shots they wanted, the public address announcer basically said "We're going to play *Wild Thing*, so everyone stand up, cheer and pretend that Charlie Sheen is coming in from the bullpen".

At that '96 home run derby, Barry Bonds won to further cement his status as a universally admired baseball player. I'm sure everything turned out great for him. I also remember Jeff Bagwell putting one almost in the 700 level in left field. It's a shame this event is so worn out today because it was awesome when I was a kid. But once you've seen 10,000 home runs, I guess it loses its luster.

The All-Star Game itself was quite a spectacle. Before the game, we saw something happen in the outfield as the American League was taking its team picture. Later on, we found out that White Sox reliever Roberto Hernandez had stumbled while stepping down from one of the risers, threw his arm up to balance himself and hit Cal Ripken Jr. in the face, breaking the Iron Man's nose. An MLB record consecutive games streak almost ended because of this. But Cal played in that game and carried on for a few more years before finally taking a seat.

The Phillies had just one representative at the game that year, which was an annual occurrence. In 1996, it was closer Ricky Botallico because there really wasn't anyone else to pick from. Having a relief pitcher selected as your lone representative is the biggest slap in the face a team can get because it shows that none of your regular lineup or rotation is good enough. Still, Ricky Bo received a nice ovation and got into the game for an inning at one point. Local boy Mike Piazza, then of the Dodgers, homered and was named the MVP in the NL's 6-0 win. I was still a few years away from hating Piazza, as he would go on to become a Met. He failed to win a World Series though, so no harm no foul. Amazingly, the NL wouldn't win another All-Star Game until 2010.

During this time period, the Francona years, the Phillies were flat-out terrible. As I said, he wasn't completely at fault because of the measly options available to him, but his "player's manager" attitude and inexperience clearly didn't help. He had a couple useful pieces but not enough to field a competitive team, especially when he would baby the likes of Bobby Abreu and Scott Rolen (more on Rolen later).

Going to Phillies games still retained most of its fun, but it was pretty disheartening to cheer them on in a dilapidated old stadium where empty seats far outnumbered occupied ones and the end result was likely to be a very undesirable one. This is why a handful of people could dominate whole sections with signs, stupid dances and whatever lewd behavior PhanaVision was able to capture on any given night.

Near the end of Francona's seemingly never-ending reign of terror, the organization finally pulled the trigger on a trade to send Curt Schilling out of town. Schilling was the last vestige of the '93 World Series squad but wasn't doing any good for anyone taking the mound every fifth day for such a bad team. The trade to Arizona would give him a chance to win a title in the latter part of his career. What came back in return was…well, it was a steaming pile. A true masterpiece pulled off by Phillies GM Ed Wade. It was a harbinger of things to come.

After the 2000 season, the team finally gave everyone around here some hope by finally giving Francona the axe. And much to the delight of people like Mike's dad, Larry Bowa was hired in his stead. He had been begging for Bowa for about three years and was getting his wish. I frankly didn't care who was at the helm, as long as it wasn't Francona. I was convinced that non-handshaking bum was never going to win anything. The Phillies were immediately better under Bowa and got back to being relevant. Not quite playoff level, but getting there. And some of their newfound success was due in large part to the play of exciting young shortstop Jimmy Rollins.

In the offseason following Rollins' solid rookie season, I was able to meet him when the Phillies' winter caravan came to a convention center in Wilmington. I was 16 at the time and was basically eye to eye with Jimmy. It's amazing to think of what he was able to do with such a slight frame. I timidly asked him to sign a baseball for me and he replied "Sure thing, big man". This was awesome for me. He handed it back and I told him to "Keep doing what you're doing" like I was a coach or something. He answered "All right, I will". Unfortunately I destroyed all value of said baseball moments later by getting fellow rookie Brandon Duckworth to sign it also.

Duckworth had compiled a 3-2 record in a late-season callup, looking very good in the process. But he would go on to spend just two more years with the Phillies, posting an ERA over 5.00 and only winning 20 more games in his major league career. So yeah, bad decision on my part. I did have another ball with me and after getting beleaguered reliever (but former All-Star) Ricky Botallico to sign it for some reason, I decided it would be my "crap ball" and set my sights on Ed Wade to autograph it as well. I found him in the middle of a room, nowhere near a table or anywhere else to put his drink down, so he had to sit it on the floor. He signed for a few other people before me and then did for me as well. It was definitely not one of the greatest thrills of my life, but I really enjoyed what came next.

I was still in the vicinity after getting his autograph and he was signing for someone else when a little kid came whizzing by out of nowhere and knocked his drink over. I remember Ed Wade having virtually no reaction, just a "this is my life" dead stare that I imagine was his permanent expression while watching his team's games. Instead, he robotically took a knee and began scooping the spilled ice off the carpet and back into the cup. And so I stood watching the general manager of a professional sports team clean up a spilled cocktail. Some would see it as a humanizing moment. I was just embarrassed for ol' Ed and the Phillies. It was pretty mundane, but still, it was bizarre and I'll never forget how sad it seemed, like a microcosm of being a Philadelphia fan at that point in time.

During this same late-90's/early 2000's time period, I got really into hockey. I mean, insane. The Flyers weren't any good when I was a little kid (save for 2 Cup Final appearances before my 3rd birthday, not that I remember those). With the arrival of Eric Lindros, though, things changed. It took a few years, but by 1995 the Flyers and I finally found each other as the cosmic ballet brought us together in a full unwavering embrace that only the grave will one day separate. I do admit to also having a bit of a thing for the Montreal Canadiens around then. I don't know if it was the allure of the whole French-Canadian thing or the awesome jerseys or the storied franchise history, but I liked them, especially goaltender Patrick Roy. I had always been drawn to the goaltending position and he was the best in the league, so it was a natural fit. But this waned over time, and I have been 110% behind just the Flyers for a long while.

The NHL almost killed itself with a lockout after the 1994 season ended, then finally came back with an abbreviated 48-game schedule for the following campaign. What followed was a thrill-a-minute, action-packed slate of games and a memorable season for the orange and black. The tone was set early in the year by the trade (with those Canadiens) that brought John LeClair and Eric Desjardins to town. The Flyers were finally getting good!

Down the stretch of that season, my dad sprang for primo seats at the Spectrum and I got to see Patrick Roy and the Canadiens in person for the first time. I was so pumped for that game. I came away happy as Roy was his usual self but the Flyers still won 3-2. The biggest thrill of that night, however, was meeting Bernie Parent for the first time. He was signing autographs between periods and I took my program (unfortunately featuring rookie defenseman Chris Therien on the cover) for him to autograph.

So I met Bernie, shook his hand, got him to sign the program, and my dad took a photo. A photo of the greatest goalie in Flyers history. And me. Wearing my Canadiens jersey. Bernie made me feel better about it by telling me he was actually from Montreal, which blew me away because kids don't ever think about a team's players being from somewhere else. We are all pretty dumb as kids I guess. What a night, though. I tacked that picture on my bedroom door and it stayed there for over a decade. In the years since, I have come to a conclusion about Mr. Bernard Marcel Parent. He is #1. And I don't just mean the number he wore on the ice. He is the best. Period. Don't even think of fighting me on this because you're going to lose. Bernie. #1. The greatest. Forever.

That sprint of a '95 season lasted into the third round when the Flyers lost in the East Final to the upstart Devils. I was crushed. It stung even more after the Devils easily swept the heavily-favored Red Wings to win the Stanley Cup. I couldn't believe that franchise had managed to win it all. They paraded the Cup around their arena's parking lot because they didn't play for a city so much as for an exit off the highway. But I was at least hopeful that the Flyers were here to stay. And if they were going to be a good team for a long time, they had to win a Cup at some point soon. Right?

The following year the Flyers ran over everybody in the East and were the #1 seed heading into the playoffs. They dispatched the Lightning, who were making their first ever playoff appearance, in round 1. It took a lot more effort than anyone expected, though. In the second round they met the upstart Panthers. Notice a pattern? Florida, another recent expansion team in just their third season in the NHL, was also making their first playoff appearance. The series was a mind-boggling nightmare. Led by their shutdown boring defense and backstopped by the goaltending of John "Beezer" Vanbiesbrouck, the Panthers beat the Flyers in six games. Florida would go on to the Stanley Cup Final before being smoked by Colorado, which was a small consolation.

That closed the doors on the Spectrum for Flyers hockey and also slammed a window shut on the chances of what was probably the Flyers' best team from that era. With Lindros and the Legion of Doom at their finest and a pretty solid supporting cast, it was extremely disappointing that the team didn't make any headway after their emergence the previous year. As a new day dawned for the Flyers at the CoreStates Center for the 1996-97 season, the team posted its usual solid point total and then hoped to kick it into high gear for the playoffs. The opening round brought the Penguins, I team I hadn't yet learned to hate. Mario Lemieux was said to be retiring after the season, his body too broken down from all of the various health problems suffered throughout his magnificent career.

I was at Game 1. With the Flyers up midway through the game, fans were already breaking out the "Start up the golf cart!" taunts for Lemieux and company. It was way too premature, but still great. The Flyers went on to have a relatively easy time with the Pens, winning in five games. Lemieux had his moment, though, scoring a meaningless goal on a breakaway late in Pittsburgh's only win of the series. It was truly the only good thing that Penguins fans have ever deserved.

The Flyers drew the Buffalo Sabres in the second round and caught a huge break as goaltender Dominik Hasek was out due to injury and was also serving a suspension from an altercation with a reporter. They would take full advantage of his replacement, Steve "Panty" Shields, winning in five games once again. Then, it was time for the Rangers, a team loaded with aging stars aiming for one last shot at the Cup. We had tickets for Game 5, so while I would never hope for the Flyers to lose any games, the ideal situation would have been for them to take three of the first four so that I could be in attendance as they looked to clinch and return to the Stanley Cup Final for the first time in a decade. And despite a Wayne Gretzky hat trick leading the Rangers to a Game 2 win, the Flyers did indeed win three of four. Game 4 was an instant classic, with Lindros scoring the biggest goal of his NHL career in the waning seconds to give the Flyers the win.

That set the stage just as I had envisioned it for Game 5. The Flyers would fall behind in the first period, but they came back to get the win and send me and the rest of the fans into a frenzy. This was it. They were going to do it. I was even going to Game 1 of the Stanley Cup Final. Pre-pubescent me was jumping out of my skin and planning a summer wardrobe that was going to consist entirely of Flyers' championship t-shirts. Then the Detroit Red Wings came to town.

At said Game 1, the Flyers were down by a goal early in the third when Steve Yzerman teed one up from the blue line and blew it by Ron Hextall for the insurance goal and proverbial dagger. You could hear a pin drop in the building. Crap. This wasn't going to be easy. These guys are good. The Flyers needed to pick it up big time. But it never happened. Detroit dismantled the Flyers in four straight, and that was that. I was beside myself. How could this team seemingly just quit the way it had? Rather, "choke", as head coach Terry Murray would famously say.

As it turns out, getting their heads kicked in by the Red Wings was the beginning of the end for that team. First round exits in '98 and '99 were once again discouraging, but even more importantly, major fissures began to develop between the team's captain and the organization. Eric Lindros had been taking hit after hit and was a frequent absentee from the lineup, much to the chagrin of Flyers GM Bob Clarke and the fans. To make matters worse, Lindros had freakishly even suffered a collapsed lung and missed the stretch drive and entire playoffs in 1999.

Things came to a head (no pun intended) in the 1999-2000 season, as the Flyers got their act back together and made another run to the Eastern Final, largely without Lindros, who had played just 55 games during the regular season and had missed the first two rounds. That second round, of course, was highlighted by Keith Primeau's winning goal in the 5th overtime in Pittsburgh. Regrettably, it was a school night and I only managed to stay awake through the third overtime. I do remember, however, going to bed with the radio on and being briefly awakened by the exuberant goal call. I smiled and fell back asleep.

After the Flyers got done dispatching the Penguins, it was the Devils again standing in their way. I didn't have a good feeling about it at all, but the Flyers managed to claim a 3-1 series lead (sans Lindros) and headed back home with a chance to clinch in Game 5. I was going to the game with a trip to the Final just one win away, shades of 1997 all over again. "Tonight's the night!" people were exclaiming in our section just before the pre-game introductions. But the Flyers fell flat on their faces and lost 4-1. My stomach was churning again with that feeling of dread.

It turned out to be well-founded. Lindros actually returned the next game and scored the Flyers' lone goal in a 2-1 loss, so it was back to Philadelphia for a winner-take-all Game 7. What ensued was perhaps the single most demoralizing moment in my life as a Philadelphia sports fan and in the history of the Flyers franchise.

By this point in time, many had soured on Eric Lindros. I was on the fence. The team didn't seem to "need" him anymore and his injuries and spats with the front office (specifically Clarke) were an unwanted distraction. I myopically agreed with the team because, as a naïve kid, they could do no wrong in my eyes. Lindros should have sucked it up and played, I agreed, and his parents needed to stop meddling. Really, everyone was just hoping to get whatever we could out of him before it was too late, but it was plain that the end was nigh.

So when Lindros cut across the middle of the ice during that fateful Game 7, head down, it was almost unsurprising that he was obliterated by Scott Stevens. That hit, and the image of Lindros motionless on the ice afterward, said it all. It was a microcosm for the Flyers' shattered dreams, an apropos bookend for a decade's worth of hope and then subsequent failure. That the Flyers lost the game and finished their collapse was more or less secondary. Following that hit, it was a foregone conclusion. The team and its fans were broken.

At this point in my life, I believe I was still observing the annual tradition of crying/throwing a tantrum when the Flyers got eliminated from the playoffs. After this one, I was just numb. I felt like someone, specifically Scott Stevens, had ripped out my guts. This guy. The NHL will tell you he's one of their 100 greatest players ever, but with today's rules and increased awareness about head injuries, Stevens would get suspended for every other bodycheck that he threw. His headhunting, shoulder-to-the-brain tactics were an embarrassment for the league, who admittedly should have done way more to protect the health of their star players like Lindros.

If the Big E had started his career ten or fifteen years later, when the league was realizing it needed to outlaw headshots and shore up player safety to provide the best product for its fans, maybe he would have fully realized his potential. But he didn't and ultimately fell well short of what we all expected. Of course he did. Welcome to being a Flyers fan. F my life.

That was, as well all know, Lindros' last game as a Flyer. He refused to get back on the ice for them and, after a year off, was traded to the Rangers. The divorce was complete. The fact that he went to the Flyers' bitterest rival in exchange for a sack of garbage (other than Kim Johnsson) made it hurt even worse. Two more weak first round exits by the Flyers in the seasons immediately following the Stevens hit only added to the misery. I was totally in the doldrums as a Flyers fan.

During all this time, the man who was probably the best athlete in town played for the only local team I haven't mentioned here yet. Allen Iverson was a one-man show who burst onto the scene in 1996. The 76ers improved steadily for four straight seasons. Then, in 2000-01,

Iverson put them on his back and took them to the NBA Finals against the Lakers, the Sixers' three-time Finals nemeses from the 1980's.

Everybody seemed to be enjoying the ride except for me. I was so soured on sports, with the Phillies and Eagles stinking and the Flyers' never-ending playoff failures, that I even emailed a local TV station to express my annoyance that broadcasts started off with Sixers coverage instead of "real news". I guess I just can't stand to see people happy when I'm not able to get completely on board with it. The bandwagon mentality just isn't for me. Deep down I was probably happy that at least some team in town was doing well, although I'd be fairly disappointed if the team I cared about the least ending up winning the first Philly title of my lifetime.

Well, those concerns didn't last long. Despite a thrilling Game 1 victory in LA, which I stayed up to watch and was actually kind of excited about, the Sixers dropped four straight to put an end to a magical season. Iverson would never again get past the second round in his Sixers career. Years later, A.I. would be the central figure in one of the few great 76ers moments in my life. While working for ArenaVision (more on that later), I got to be on the court before the game as he returned to Philadelphia for the first time as a member of the visiting Nuggets. I was mere feet away holding my cameraman's cable (no jokes, please) as he was introduced, acknowledged the fans, and kissed the logo at center court. It was quite a moment and was one of the loudest ovations I have ever heard in that building, whatever it was called at the time.

So, Philadelphia sports had entered the 21st century as a mixed bag. The Phillies were a mess and there didn't seem to be too much hope for the immediate future. The Flyers were stuck in neutral, good but never able to get over the hump. And at the time, the 76ers seemed to be on the rise and capable of being the first team to break through and deliver that elusive championship that the city had been seeking my whole life. Meanwhile, in BirdLand, things were really heating up. A team was ready to take the city back and establish itself as the #1 game in town for years to come.

*

3.

SAME CRAP, DIFFERENT CENTURY

It was year two of the McNabb/Reid era, and I was getting legitimately excited about the Eagles. The Phillies and even the Flyers were taking a back seat in my mind. After expected growing pains in his first season as coach, Big Red led the Birds to an 11-5 mark in 2000, and the team was headed back to the playoffs for the first time in four years. In their opening game, they dismantled Tampa Bay. Ha, Tampa. Those guys would never win anything. Then they hit the road for a date with the Giants. But there would be no Miracle at the Meadowlands #2 (at least not yet) and they lost 20-10. It stung, but it was a really promising season. And thankfully the Giants would eventually lose in the Super Bowl. Those guys would never win anything either.

The town and all of its fans were positively bleeding green. I'm sure that episodes of Eagles mania had come and gone throughout the area over the years, but it was about to hit new levels. The following season, the Eagles posted an identical 11-5 record but it was enough to win the division this time. They again opened the playoffs with a win over the Bucs. Too easy, we just had those guys' number. Next up was a road matchup against the Bears in round two. The Eagles would pull off the upset, stifling Chicago to earn a trip to the NFC Championship Game. Waiting for them were the Rams and the "Greatest Show on Turf", an offense seemingly impossible to contain.

I think we were all in the "just happy to be here, but let's not embarrass ourselves" mentality for this one. As with most big games throughout my life, I can tell you where I was when I watched it. This time, it was at my friend Steve's house, and we piled into his room as we tried to wish our way to a Super Bowl appearance. As usual, Steve ordered about 7 pizzas and 100 wings. For four teenagers.

The Eagles actually led at halftime but relinquished the lead late in the third quarter. They fell behind by two possessions, but a McNabb TD run (remember when he did that?) with just under three minutes left narrowed the gap to 29-24. The Eagles got the ball back late but ran out of time and downs to fall just short against a superior adversary. They hung tough all game.

Again, it was disappointing. But we weren't throwing things over it. We saw the effort. We were so happy about how good the season had been and were expecting to take the next step in the following season. Maybe we were on the cusp of being some kind of juggernaut. We were wrong.

It was during this time period that the city finally stopped sitting on its hands and broke ground on two new stadiums. Pittsburgh had received its funding at the same time as Philadelphia and both of their new facilities were already open. Clearly they had to put all of their efforts into improving the viability of the Steelers and Pirates because they didn't give a damn about their hockey team out there. But I digress. It was going to be a new era in Philadelphia. The hockey/basketball arena was only a couple years old, and we were about to get two more new world-class facilities to boot.

The Phillies were still trying to wash off the stink of the Francona years and were seeing some improvement, although they were seemingly still a ways off from contender status. In 2001, Larry Bowa's first season, they saw a 21-win increase from the previous year and narrowly missed the playoffs. Bowa won Manager of the Year honors for his efforts.

Sports had been an all-out assault on my senses up to that point of my life. But things were changing. High school was coming to a close and I was forced with the prospect of being an adult. One of these days, I may even get there. But I got a girlfriend and my interests suddenly didn't solely revolve around catching that night's Flyers or Phillies game. And I must also acknowledge the events of September 11, 2001 and their undeniable impact on every facet of life.

After the horrible tragedies of that day, everything stopped. We wondered immediately what the point of things like sports were. I recall thinking about what would happen to stand-up comedy, sitcoms, movies and anything that was supposed to make us laugh or give enjoyment of any kind. These were minor concerns in the face of dealing with the aftermath of what happened, but how was life ever going to be the same?

It turns out it never was the same, but the resilience of the people in this country was something to behold. There was an immediate wave of patriotism and goodwill like never before, although it would then give way to a new culture of fear and suspicion that quickly developed and would unfortunately end up dominating down the line. As we attempted to heal, we took a short break from things like sports before forging ahead with them.

It seemed as though everyone briefly paused to consider if we should bother with such frivolities but then decided that, yes, it was worth it. We could not and would not change our way of life in the face of evil and cowardice, and the value of sports, in a way that surprised many, was evident more than ever before. I embraced it, as did most people who were big fans before 9/11, as an important enough part of my identity and my life to continue supporting with a passion. The sense of community and togetherness that sports can foster cannot be overstated. When I look back on this time, it helps me remember to take tough losses with a proverbial grain of salt and focus on what truly matters. Of course, I still would prefer to win.

The 2002 season saw the Phillies dip back below .500. It was a season that was all over the map. In June, the team's first round pick was a left-handed pitcher named Cole Hamels. We'd hear from him later on down the road. In July, longtime broadcaster Harry Kalas got the criminally overdue honor of induction into the Baseball Hall of Fame. I was there. He was my idol. I can't tell you how much time was spent with friends recreating Harry's calls of big plays (good and bad) or making up our own dialogue in Harry's distinctive baritone. I smile just to think about what he meant to me and no doubt countless other Phillies fans. And this gives me the perfect opportunity to recount my very favorite story.

I've told it many times but I never tire of it. It was the previous year, July 9, 2001, to be exact. My friends Bill, Mike and I were enjoying a summer day at Dorney Park. And yes, I can frequently pinpoint exact dates in my life if something notable happened on them, especially when it's sports-related. This particular date is easy to do an internet search on and identify because it was the day before that year's MLB All-Star Game. In and of itself, that probably seems trivial, but it turned out to be a key factor in this story.

We were strolling through the park and headed over to Steel Force, one of my favorite roller coasters. Then, about 100 feet ahead of us and off to the right, we spied an older gentlemen just sitting on a bench doing nothing in particular. He was wearing sunglasses and was conspicuously well-dressed for an amusement park. Clearly he was just waiting for whoever he was with to finish a ride. I distinctly remember giving a quick point in his direction and joking "Hey look, it's Harry Kalas". My friends looked and let out some agreeable laughs. We continued toward the ride, getting somewhat closer to the man on the bench, who was now directly off to our right. Without any of us breaking stride, we all agreed aloud at the same time that, holy crap, that might actually be Harry Kalas.

In an unusually bold move for me, I actually made the executive decision to approach. I had to be sure. I sidled up on his right. I couldn't tell where he was looking since he had the sunglasses on, but he didn't seem to see me coming up. A few feet away, I got the unmistakable whiff of cigars that clings to someone who smokes them at all times. I knew it! I got close and in probably the meekest voice ever said, "Excuse me, sir, are you Harry Kalas"?

He smoothly turned his head up and to his right, and with the hint of a smile, declared "Yes I am". At that point, for this 16-year old kid, the world stopped. It was just me and Harry and I couldn't be more oblivious to what was going on around me. I said something along the lines of being a huge fan of his and the team. I think I shook his hand. I was shaking, babbling, probably crapped myself. Why didn't I have a camera? Why hadn't smartphones been invented yet? At some point, my friends must have seen how I was acting and rushed up to join. Harry endured the onslaught of excited teenagers and couldn't have been nicer.

We buttered him up right good. But it was all legit. We loved Harry. He WAS the Phillies, and we told him so. He was there that day with his family since the league was on its All-Star break (ding ding, told you there was a good reason I mentioned that) and he didn't get many of these free days throughout the baseball season. While talking to Harry, my mind went to that year's upcoming Hall of Fame inductions and the fact that I was beside myself that Harry had not gotten the call yet. The Hall annually presents one broadcaster with the Ford C. Frick Award, and that year it was going to some guy who had been announcing Marlins games in Spanish for all of about eight years. Way to go, voters. And so I felt the need to tell Harry that he had been robbed and that, when he did get in, I was going to Cooperstown for the induction. He found that to be very nice, said it would be an honor to get in, and was generally just awesome about everything.

Our whole encounter with Harry the K probably only lasted about 90 seconds and I'm amazed that nobody else horned in on us and came over to bother him. But, short as it may have been, that moment will be etched for all time in my memory and my heart. We composed ourselves enough to go ride the roller coaster, which was a huge letdown after the thrill that we had just had. We actually passed by Harry once more on the way off the ride as we made our way to a different part of the park. I think we giddily waved goodbye to him. He acknowledged us and asked my friend how the ride was. And that was that, my brief experience with Harry and the only time I would ever meet the man and legend. It was simply amazing to me and the two best friends I got to share it with.

The following year, Harry did finally get that Hall call, and it didn't take much pestering from me to get my parents to go to induction weekend. Ozzie Smith, whose last All-Star Game was the 1996 affair I had seen at the Vet, was also being honored. Great player, great speech. But all of my focus was on Harry. I was so happy. The Hall of Fame weekend took only the slightest ding when word came out that the Phillies had traded disgruntled third baseman Scott Rolen. Everyone had had it with him by that point anyway. What a miserable human being. You haven't heard the last of what I have to say about Scott Rolen, but we'll come around to that later.

Once the games had concluded that year, the Phillies began preparations for their final season at the Vet. They really needed to do something to shake it up and show that they were serious players. In December, they did just that. They signed David Bell. But as great as that was, they somehow made an even bigger move when they inked elite slugger Jim Thome. This was amazing; the Phillies might actually have a fearsome offense in 2003 and beyond. And a lot of the credit for the Thome signing has to go to Scott Rolen, who the Phillies would have otherwise wasted a good chunk of the Thome money on if he hadn't whined his way out of town. Thanks, Scott!

Getting Thome seemed especially important after the Phillies had supposedly just missed out on getting Tom Glavine, who had agreed to a contract with the Mets the day before. I remember the general bummed-out feeling around town in the brief time between the two signings. The Mets and their fans were laughing at us. They really put one over on the Phillies! Yeah, we'll check back in later and let you know how that one worked out.

At this point, I was well into my freshman year at La Salle University. The draw of going to college in Philadelphia, mostly due to my love of the sports teams, had appealed to me for a long time. I chose La Salle because of its impressive communication program, college TV station, and the myriad potential options available to me in a large market where I was hoping to someday catch on in broadcasting, sports media or some other similar field there.

I was a homebody and would still come back to good ol' Delaware to see my girlfriend and other buddies on most weekends, but I was loving the close proximity to my teams. On days when I had an early class, I would be up and out of the dorm complex in enough time to grab a free copy of the *Philadelphia Daily News* that sat in a bin by the exit before they were all taken. At least, I think they were free. It was great to read in often excruciating detail about the previous day's Eagles and Flyers games. And I made sure to always read everything written by longtime Phillies beat writer Bill Conlin. Some days I would be out of luck and have to grab an *Inquirer* instead. But I would occasionally go and pay for a *Daily News* at John's sausage cart on the corner of 20th and Olney if I really wanted to read it on a given day. Man, that sausage was good.

The college experience was taking up a lot of my time, as you would expect, but I was still able to cram as much sports time as I could into my busy educational and social schedule. Of the utmost importance were the Eagles, playing their final season at Veterans Stadium. My dad and I attended the final regular season Eagles game at the Vet, a win over the Redskins. I had only been to two Eagles games in my life prior to that, so I'm sorry if you wanted to go to that game and couldn't get tickets. My bad.

It was a fine season for a surging Eagles club, as they went 12-4 and earned a first round bye. In the playoffs, they would take care of Michael Vick and the Falcons and earn their second consecutive berth in the NFC Championship Game. But this time, the Eagles were playing at home. Even better, their opponent would be Tampa Bay, whose all-time record in "cold weather" games was about 0-108. Or something like that. And we had just ended their season two years in a row to boot. Oh man.

Home for the weekend and watching the game at Mike's house, we were all pumped to see the Eagles make the Super Bowl for the first time in our lives. Mike's dad wouldn't have to refer to it as the "Stupid Bowl" that year, as he always did since the Eagles never made it. Brian Mitchell nearly returned the opening kickoff for a touchdown, finally being brought down at Tampa's 26-yard line. Excitement was almost reaching a fever pitch already.

Two plays later, Duce Staley ripped off a touchdown run and everyone around here exploded in a seizure of elation. We all flew up off the couch in a simultaneous eruption of screams and high-fives. This was it. Most memorably, Mike, at the top of his lungs, bellowed "The rout is on!" This will stick with me for as long as I live. There was no reason to doubt this.

It would have gained universal acceptance at that moment. My dad was at the game and would later tell me that the Tampa fans sitting in front of him were already turtling up and admitting defeat at this point. Like the Eagles against the Rams the previous year, they were just happy to be there and were hoping to make it out with their dignity and their lives.

Tampa responded with a field goal on their first drive, but that was a trivial occurrence. Then, late in the first quarter, the undisputed turning point of the game occurred. Joe Jurevicius took a short pass from Brad Johnson and was able to pull off a 71-yard catch and run before mercifully being hauled down by Brian Dawkins at the Eagles' 5-yard line. What a complete and total defensive breakdown. The history books will say that the Vet came down the following year via explosive charges, but in truth it was this play that did it. Two plays later, everyone's last-resort second RB in their fantasy league, Mike Alstott, plunged into the endzone and the Bucs had the lead. The Eagles would actually tie it up in the second quarter, but a late score by Tampa had them down 17-10 heading into halftime.

We were all nervous, and the only thing that distracted us at this point was Ja Rule's halftime performance, undoubtedly one of the all-time worst. The fans absolutely let him have it. If the Eagles were up by two touchdowns like they should have been, nobody would have given a damn. But the fear and the anger was bubbling up. This was our year, and this team had better not blow it.

I wish I could tell you that the Eagles fought the good fight and the Bucs let them be. I wish I could tell you that – but sports is no fairy-tale world. This was all just part of our routine as Philadelphia sports fans. It got deep into the fourth without any further scoring save for a Tampa field goal, so the Eagles' deficit was ten points. Desperation time. We all knew it wasn't going to work out, but it didn't have to be as painful as it ended up being. Ronde Barber's 92-yard interception return was the final bitter pill to swallow. The Eagles era at Veterans Stadium was over. Sadly, given all of the pain and bad teams over the years, it was probably appropriate. I slunk back up to school that night. Numbness again.

At this point, it was time to focus my attention back on the Phillies' swansong at the Vet and the Flyers' inevitable spring letdown. But once playoff hockey got underway for the orange and black, it was actually exciting that particular year. Facing Toronto in the first round, the teams traded blows and the series saw several overtime games. In one pivotal contest, Mark

Recchi's triple-overtime winner sent me dancing around the dorm in my undershirt and boxers. I would have been embarrassed if I wasn't so excited. In the end, it all came down to a Game 7 at home again, just like in 2000 against the Devils. Granted, this was the first round, but it still had the feeling of a game that the Flyers desperately needed to win in order to stay relevant.

Now, I've never been to a seventh game of the Stanley Cup Playoffs in person. And I probably never will be. The likely fee for such a ticket and a thorough cost/benefit analysis of the price and outcome (win or loss) really makes me skittish about that kind of an investment. It would simply be too much. First off, I probably would have a 50/50 shot of even making it out of the first period without suffering a fatal heart attack. And even after that, the combined buy-in from my soul and my wallet might literally kill me if they were to lose such a game.

On the night of this particular Game 7, I was watching from the relative comfort of my dorm room. I was keyed up while at the same time feeling like something would inevitably crush me as usual. But to my surprise and amazement, the Flyers actually came out and smoked the Maple Leafs to advance. What a relief. It was the team's first Game 7 win since 1989, which I was too young to remember. What a feeling. Bring on Ottawa! But…The Flyers would lose in six games.

Dammit. Another season wasted. In truth, the team probably finished right about where they should have, but I was conditioned at this point to just dismiss it as a letdown yet again. Maybe next year. Yeah yeah. On to the Phillies. Led by Thome and his 47 dingers (one short of Mike Schmidt's team record), the team hung around for a large chunk of the year but ultimately fell five games short of a playoff berth. Chase Utley bashing a grand slam as his first major league hit was one of the year's biggest highlights. And I was able to go to the final game at the Vet, an otherwise unmemorable loss to the Braves. Still (and I felt like I said this after every year in the Bowa era), the team was tracking upward. The next season at a new stadium was going to be special.

Overlapping all of this sports craziness was the beginning of my illustrious career in television. The timid kid off on his own at college took a little while to adapt, but I finally motivated myself enough to get involved with our school's television station, La Salle 56. Some years later, it would become "La Salle TV" but it'll always be 56 to me and will be henceforth be referred to as such.

There were several interesting pre-existing shows to work on, but of course I wanted to focus mostly on the sports programs. We had *SportsLine*, which covered La Salle athletics, and I did help out on that show from time to time, but my passion didn't lie in a straightforward news desk style of broadcasting. Instead, I threw most of my efforts into *Sports Talk Philadelphia*, which I have always described as a *Sports Reporters*-type of roundtable discussion.

The panelists, usually four of them, would talk about the local sports scene, breaking down highlights and offering insights into upcoming games and the season as a whole. There was room for debate, there was room for humor, and there was room for personality and passion. Sign me up. Of course, as a lowly freshman, I had to begin by working behind the scenes. I would bide my time, oh yes, but I would have my day. Truthfully, crewing shows like this were a lot of fun because it offered experience and introduced me to this strange new world without overwhelming me with the responsibility and pressure that came with being on air, editing packages and otherwise producing the program. But I wanted to take the helm by junior year and set that as a goal for myself.

As sophomore me was just getting over the final goodbye to Veterans Stadium, the Eagles were enjoying their first season at shiny new Lincoln Financial Field across the parking lot. After having the door to their old home slammed shut by Tampa, the Eagles opened the new building with another game against the Bucs. Again it sucked, as they lost 17-0 to complete bookend embarrassments at the hands of the defending Super Bowl champs. Then, after falling to 0-2 and seemingly on life support, the Birds ripped off 11 wins in 12 games to reassert themselves as the team to beat in the NFC once again while Tampa fell apart and finished 7-9. At least we didn't have to deal with those guys.

Sick as a dog, I was watching from my dorm room as the Eagles took on Brett Favre and the Packers in the playoffs. They were given all they could handle, but in the end miraculously pulled off the famed 4th and 26 conversion as Freddie Mitchell made the one and only good play of his career. Favre then offered up one of his patented jump ball interceptions in overtime, leading directly to the Eagles' win. I think I let out a stifled "yay" as I alternated between burning up and shivering in my dorm bed, watching on a small TV from across the room. Hopefully I was going to be alive for the NFC Championship Game the following week. In retrospect, maybe the alternative would have been better.

That year's spoiler would be the Carolina Panthers, who waltzed into the Linc and terrorized a banged-up Donovan McNabb, sacking him five times and intercepting him on four occasions while holding him to just 100 yards passing in a demoralizing 14-3 Panthers win. The lone highlight of my day was watching my friend's college roommate, frothing in anger, pick up a gel air freshener and hurl it with all his might through the paper-thin dining room wall of their off-campus house. I believe they drywalled the hole up some months later to avoid losing their deposit, but it will always smell pine fresh in there. The Eagles, not so much. Was this team ever going to finish the job? We'd have to wait another year to see.

*

4.

THIS IS SOMETHING NEW

Seeing the Eagles dead and buried yet again following this latest disappointment, a lot of "fans" in the city were probably too depressed to even turn their sights to the Phillies. But I was really in need of it. And I was pretty excited that the team was opening a brand spanking new ballpark for the 2004 season. Not only that, but they were getting new digs down at their spring training site in Clearwater, Florida. What a perfect time to make my first ever trip down there.

And so we took a family vacation to the Sunshine State, ostensibly to escape the doldrums of late winter in the mid-Atlantic region. But really it was just to see the Phillies. Bright House Networks Field, as it was then called, was pretty impressive. It would also serve as the new home of the just-rebranded Clearwater Threshers, the Phils' single-A affiliate. And it definitely wasn't your run-of-the-mill minor league ballpark, at least not like one you'd see up this way, which of course was necessary since the big club needed a whole complex around it for all their spring training needs.

We had tickets for the first two games at the park, strategically scheduled against the Yankees in order to pull in every last dollar they could. Part of the attraction was also being able to stroll the surrounding facilities and watch the players take part in drills and practices that you wouldn't otherwise be privy to during a typical regular season baseball experience. Maybe you'd even be lucky enough to see someone get hit in the groin. I was.

A large group of Phillies pitchers were taking fielding practice on one of the back fields, as one of the coaches hit grounders to them. I don't know how often a reliever will be fielding ground balls hit from 100 feet away in a game situation, but that's why I'm not in the big leagues I guess. Anyway, a couple players fielded grounders cleanly and without incident and then rotated out. Then, in stepped Amaury Telemaco.

Telemaco was your archetypal below-average reliever and last resort starting pitcher when you were out of options. He had come to the team in 1999 after being picked up off waivers. In a bizarre series of moves, he would sign five separate contracts with the Phillies over the course of his major league career. Three of the contracts were after he had hit free agency and two of them were after the Phillies had released him the previous week. Obviously there were some kind of deals worked out with him and his agent to sit tight while the Phillies shoehorned him back onto the roster after making some other transactions. You might even be tempted to call it collusion but for the fact that he wasn't any good and no other team wanted him.

Anyhow, on this fateful spring day, Telemaco took his position on the infield dirt. The coach swung and hit a pretty hard two-hopper out towards him. It looked ordinary, but the ball caught the lip of the grass and drastically changed its trajectory. It had become a heat-seeking missile. There was a thud. Telemaco was brought down in agony. You couldn't have placed the shot more perfectly if you had a laser scope. Right in the balls. And based on the sound, you knew it had only hit a few centimeters of fabric. No cup. As he writhed and struggled for breath, so did his teammates who were falling over laughing. Great camaraderie there. It was pretty funny, but I felt for the guy. Thankfully, there was no long-term damage because he was his normal subpar self that year.

As for the games themselves, they weren't as exciting as a guy getting drilled in the junk, but at least we enjoyed nice weather and broke the winter-long baseball dry spell. For the first game, we had pretty good seats about 20 rows back behind home plate. We were there well before the game to take everything in and it was still sparsely populated when I spied *Daily News* writer Bill Conlin a few rows down in front of us.

As I mentioned before, I read everything that Conlin wrote and was a big fan. I had already bought a program complete with scorecard (yes, I was going to keep score for a spring training game) and could think of nothing better than having Mr. Conlin sign the lineup page in it. He had been writing about the team and Philadelphia sports in general since the 1960's, so it would have some meaning behind it.

He seemed almost surprised that someone wanted him to sign something, but he was happy to do so. It was a pleasant encounter and I was glad to have met him. Plus, I doubt anyone else has his autograph on the inaugural program from that stadium. In 2011, he would be honored by the Baseball Hall of Fame for his decades of fine writing about the sport, an accolade which was well deserved. But the last few years of his life were spent in controversy that I shan't comment on here. Suffice it to say, I was dismayed at how everything played out. It was yet another pointed reminder that sometimes we can be far more disappointed by the people that shape our sports experiences than by the teams simply losing games on the field.

This solemn digression aside, the whole spring training experience was a lot of fun, and I have to find a way to get back down there one of these years. I wasn't old enough to drink on that trip and really feel like I missed out. I've heard there's nothing like hanging at the tiki bar and throwing back a few. And maybe occasionally checking in on the game. It's the best way to watch baseball.

On the night we came back to Philadelphia, the Flyers were playing a home game against Ottawa. Nothing special there. But there had been an ugly incident when the teams had played each other the week before, and the Flyers were out for blood in this one. We got home in the middle stages of the game and were able to catch almost all of the carnage that unfolded on TV as the two teams set an NHL record for penalty minutes in a game. It was awesome. Wish I was there. Still, it provided a nice punctuation mark to my spring training excursion and welcomed me back to reality.

A few weeks later, of course, it was time to open the Phillies' new home. I'm not big on opening day baseball because the early April weather is usually lousy and the Phillies typically lose, also because of lousiness. But this one was too big to pass up. Prior to the game, they had a rapid fire unveiling of statues around the stadium. The Schmidt and Carlton ceremonies would predictably be mobbed, so my dad and I figured our best chance to actually have a good view was to head over to the Robin Roberts statue.

We got there a few minutes before the scheduled ceremony time and were able to get a spot right behind the rope about 20 feet away from Robin and Phillies broadcaster Scott Graham for the unveiling. Even though that statue is the most under-acknowledged one in the park and Roberts' contributions themselves are just a historical footnote for all but the oldest of Phillies fans, it was a moment that I'll always remember.

Incidentally, when Roberts passed away on May 6, 2010, I was in the car with my dad on the way to a Phillies game when we heard the news. By the time we arrived, the base of Robin's statue was already draped in black and a smattering of flowers laid at his feet. We paid our respects as well. He played long before my time, but he remains largely unchallenged as the greatest right-handed pitcher in team history. So, the next time you're at Citizens Bank Park, throw a glance Robin's way as you walk by and take a second to say thanks.

During the Roberts statue unveiling, I also took note that I'm about as tall as Scott Graham, which is not saying much for him. Height aside, I thought Graham was great for the Phillies and would make an excellent successor for Harry the K whenever he decided to hang 'em up. It seemed to me like he was being groomed for it and would carry on the Phillies' rich broadcasting legacy. But after the 2006 season, his contract was not renewed for reasons never really made clear to me. Disappointments were now extending to the broadcast booth. Enough already.

And so the first opening day at Citizens Bank Park was finally at hand. And no, I don't count those crappy "on deck" games they play in Philadelphia. They're just one final spring training cash grab and aren't official in any way. My excitement was only minimally dampened by the weather, which probably would have gotten the game canceled on any other day. It had rained hard earlier and never really stopped, petering out to a fine mist by pre-game introduction time. But the Phillies weren't going to let that stop them.

Instead, they stopped themselves. Despite Bobby Abreu hitting the first home run in the history of the park, the bats were silent in a 4-1 loss to the Reds. Oh, and did I mention that the Phillies had started the season on a 6-game road trip and had gone 1-5? So here we were, one game into a new stadium, and the team was 1-6, the season seemingly shot to hell already. So Philly, yet again. Other than the pageantry, I wish I hadn't even gone to the home opener. The weather was crummy and so was the team. Where have I heard that before?

It also happened during the early days of Citizens Bank Park that the Phillies faithful began the loathsome tradition of throwing visiting team's home run balls back onto the field. Aside from the fact that this is a blatant ripoff of what Cubs fans have been doing at Wrigley for years, it is also objectively stupid. Never in my life have I gotten a ball during a game, let alone a home run ball. You'd need to pry it from my cold, dead hands. Throwing it back is a waste and it could even pose an issue if a particularly inebriated fan decided to take aim at a player, coach or umpire. They'd need a good arm, but never underestimate beer strength. Anyway, I am not flexible on my position about throwing balls back. It serves no purpose and is not original in any way. End rant.

Kevin Lagowski

As the Phillies tried to dig themselves out of an early grave, it was time for that annual rite of spring: Flyers playoff disappointment. It had been your typical Flyers season, with the team headed into the playoffs as the #3 seed in the Eastern Conference, the sixth time in the last eight seasons that they had fallen in the 3-4-5 range. As usual, this was all just window dressing and the real test would be the postseason. There was also a true sense of urgency around the Flyers and the NHL as a whole. Commissioner Gary Bettman and the usual gang of idiots were in the process of letting the league's collective bargaining agreement (CBA) with the players' union die on the vine, and it was set to expire at season's end with little to no progress having been made to strike a new one. In all likelihood, the league was heading toward a work stoppage, maybe a very lengthy one.

The previous time this had occurred, 1994, the regular season had to be trimmed from its normal 82-game slate down to 48. But this situation looked to be way worse. The owners weren't budging off their demand for a salary cap in their pursuit of "cost certainty". It seemed unthinkable, but there was a distinct possibility that the whole next season could be lost. This was bad news for a Flyers team laden with veterans and in full win-now mode. Jeremy Roenick, John LeClair, Mark Recchi, Tony Amonte et al were nearing the end and it was likely that most, if not all, of the veteran core wouldn't be back if time were lost due to a lockout.

In the first round, the Flyers drew the New Jersey Devils. Even though it was a 3 vs. 6 matchup, the Flyers had finished just one point above the Devils during the year, so it was basically a coin flip. But we all knew what was coming, as the Flyers had spent a decade falling at the feet of their rivals. I was absolutely dreading going to Game 1, and I'm not even joking. The Flyers built a 2-0 lead after two periods and then extended it to 3-0 early in the third. But the Devils got two goals back in less than a minute immediately thereafter and it was pee pee pants time with over fifteen minutes still on the clock. The Devils peppered Robert Esche and ended up outshooting the Flyers 39-26. But Esche shut the door and the Flyers barely hung on to win the opener.

The Flyers would go on to win two of the next three games to take a 3-1 series lead. This was nothing new, however. The same thing had happened in 2000 and the team ended up collapsing, culminating in the Stevens-on-Lindros felony. I was attending a wedding on the afternoon of Game 5 and had mixed emotions about it. Would I be more or less on edge since I wasn't able to watch it? In those pre-smartphone days, I sauntered out of the wedding reception twice to go to the car, turn on the radio and check the score. I could hardly believe my ears. The Flyers won. They actually beat the Devils. Maybe this team was better than I thought.

Round two brought the Maple Leafs and a rematch of the previous season's epic 7-game first round series. I was on hand for another Game 1 victory in this round, and the home team proceeded to win the next three games so it game back to Philadelphia tied 2-2, when a seemingly unlikely hero would emerge. Keith Primeau had come to the Flyers in 2000 and, fifth overtime winner in that year's playoffs aside, had not met the expectations that had been placed upon him as Eric Lindros' de facto successor as #1 center and eventually the team captain. But in Game 5 against Toronto, with the Flyers at a critical juncture, Primeau played like a man possessed and netted a hat trick to power the Flyers to a 7-2 win and a 3-2 lead in the series.

In Game 6, the Flyers would not have an easy time of it, coughing up a 2-0 lead in the third. Here comes overtime, with a trip to the Eastern Conference Final on the line. What happened next was pretty incredible to watch. The Flyers were so banged up on the blueline that winger Sami Kapanen had been forced into duty as a defenseman. As he pinched to keep the puck in the offensive zone, Kapanen's unfamiliarity with the position left him in a vulnerable spot against the boards. 99% of the time you would escape this situation without incident, but unfortunately for little Sami, Maple Leafs' forward and all-time pest Darcy Tucker was bearing down on him.

Tucker absolutely leveled Kapanen and left him so dazed he couldn't make it to the bench, a no-doubt-about-it concussion. In the days before head injuries were such a big issue in sports, these cases of opposing players "getting their bell rung" were jubilant occasions for fans. "Yeah, we hurt that guy, maybe permanently! Woooooo!!!" The hit had everything going for it. Tucker made no attempt to play the puck. He left his feet to deliver the hit. He led with his elbow. He targeted the head. He was a huge a-hole. It would garner a 10-game suspension now, but in overtime of the 2004 playoffs, it was time to let 'em play. As celebrated as this hit is and always will be for Maple Leafs supporters, please notice how the YouTube videos of it don't go too much further past that play, as if something happened right after that they'd rather forget.

The immediate aftermath of Kapanen being hit was not pretty to watch. He was in a lot of trouble and hit the ice several times before basically being pulled onto the Flyers' bench. I was livid and wanted to jump through the TV and break Tucker's neck myself. But I had only to wait mere seconds for sweet retribution.

With Kapanen still hurting on the bench and the Air Canada Centre crowd in a frenzy, Jeremy Roenick broke loose on a 2-on-1. I thought there was no way that justice could be served this quickly, but JR made no mistake, wristing the winner past his former teammate Ed Belfour to stick it to Toronto. Wow! That emotional roller coaster was one hell of a ride. The Maple Leafs, one of the better teams in the East in the years leading up to this, wouldn't even make the playoffs again until 2013. The Flyers were on to the conference final. But you can keep watching the Tucker hit on your phones, Toronto. Enjoy.

The Flyers were back in the East Final for the first time in four years, this time facing the Tampa Bay Lightning. Now, Tampa was definitely a good team and had a lot of star power. But they had also been touched by an angel that particular season and had all of their regulars in their lineup. They literally suffered no important injuries all year. Meanwhile, the Flyers were hemorrhaging players left and right and were going to need an epic performance to win the series. More on that in a moment.

As for the action, the Flyers managed a split in Tampa and came home for Game 3. Tickets in hand, dad and I made our way to the Wells Fargo or Wachovia or whatever-it-was-called-then Center. The building was rocking before the game. As the time ticked down to the opening faceoff, the lights all dimmed. It was time for the all-too-familiar pre-game pump video. These things can go either way, but sometimes they were actually pretty good. On this night, I can honestly say that I witnessed the single greatest pre-game video that I've ever seen in person.

As the Flyers had not played a home game since the craziness of the Game 6 overtime in Toronto, someone in the video department had the masterstroke of an idea to juxtapose those highlights with music and clips from *Rocky*. The familiar theme from that movie played over other highlights from the playoffs before arriving to Tucker's hit on Kapanen and pairing it with Apollo Creed's knockdown of Rocky (spoiler alert) and the musical strains that accompanied it. But then, as we saw lil' Sami summoning the strength to get to the bench as well as Rocky getting up off the mat, the music began to build back up. You know the part. Sami makes it to the bench. Rocky comes back up to fight. Crescendo. Roenick scores. Other musical terms.

Rocky does some more Rockying. I'm getting all jacked up writing about this right now, this piece of video I saw one time over a decade ago. Oh my God, the crowd was going nuts.

Once the game actually started, it was a big letdown. The Flyers lost 4-1 and it was starting to feel like they were overmatched. But they bounced back for a 3-2 victory in Game 4, the winner being a shorthanded goal by captain Primeau. After losing Game 5 back in Tampa, it was do-or-die in Game 6. It had all the makings of the Flyers going quietly into the night.

But they showed some life and led 2-1 after the first, with Primeau netting a goal and an assist. Tampa scored three times in the second to take a 4-3 lead into the third. Time ticked deep into the final period and it again looked like midnight had arrived. But with just under two minutes to play, it was Primeau again. On an outstanding individual effort, he went around the net and used his long reach to stuff a loose puck across the line and tie the game. The moment was picture perfect, and it struck me immediately: If somehow the Flyers could win the Stanley Cup that season, this was the goal. This was the goal that would be always be pointed at as saving the season, as defining that team and their legacy. As defining their captain. It would be made into a statue, standing for all-time to commemorate a triumph for the team and the city. But there was still work to do. On to overtime.

And late in that extra frame, Primeau would start the play that led to the winning goal by Simon Gagne. It was Gagne's second goal of the night and Primeau's fourth point. I was delirious. If ever in my life a team had felt destined to win, this was it. All they needed was one more herculean effort. But it was all for naught. Tampa scored late in the first period to draw first blood in Game 7. Then again early in the second. Kim Johnsson got one back for the Flyers midway through regulation, but that was all that would happen.

Despite their season being on the line, the Flyers only managed 23 shots for the game. They were running on empty. Had been for some time. Not so much beaten as they were outlasted. They had done everything they possibly could. This time, the emotions inside me were different. The hurt was there, as it always is. But no anger. I was saddened for a different reason. This team deserved it. I was disappointed that they would not have a chance to play for the Stanley Cup because they poured every last ounce of effort into the fight. The final bitter pill was watching Tampa edge out the Calgary Flames in seven games to win it all. The Flyers would have won that series. Primeau's larger than life heroics and that entire 2004 team would have gone down forever in Philadelphia sports lore. Instead, they are merely a nice footnote along our unremitting path to heartbreak.

I headed back to school for my junior year at La Salle a few months later. And with the new semester came some new duties as panelist and co-executive producer for *Sports Talk Philadelphia*. To me, it was a time of great excitement. I saw it as a big chance to show off my sports knowledge and personality to a (potentially) large, mainstream audience. Was anybody actually going to watch our school station? Not really, but the opportunity was there for some good experience and a lot of fun.

And so, in September of 2004, I came out from behind the camera after two years as part of the La Salle 56 crew and started shooting my mouth off in front of it. One of the first things that my friends and I tackled was the ongoing Phillies season, one that would turn out to be solid but ultimately not good enough to snap their decade-plus streak of missing the playoffs. But by and large, our shows that fall were dominated by Eagles talk. After bringing superstar Terrell Owens on board and signing several other big names, the team was clearly all-in to grab what had eluded them in each of the last three NFC Championship Games.

Everybody in the city and seemingly everybody around football had declared the Birds as the team to beat in 2004. I know I was convinced, despite the successive gut punches the team (and more importantly its fans) had just been through the last two years. I even had a nerdy little printout up on the wall in my dorm room of their sixteen opponents and was planning on putting W's and the accompanying score up next to them after each Eagles victory. I can't remember ever having gone into any season of any sport feeling more confident. And I really have no idea why. Something felt different about this team.

The Eagles didn't even break a sweat in their first five games, and my dorm wall was starting to fill up with W's. On the show, I talked about how refreshing it was to see one of our teams FINALLY beating up on the league. I mean, not just putting up wins, but wiping the floor with its opponents. A Philadelphia team! Go figure. But then the team squeaked out a pair of wins and it was apparent that they were mortal after all. You could just feel a loss was coming, and indeed it did in a predictably ugly showing in Pittsburgh.

Still, the team was 7-1 and in great position. Any fears were allayed as they defeated all three of their divisional opponents in successive weeks by a combined score of 104-33. They followed this up with a 47-17 massacre of the Packers, who looked like they might be the Eagles' primary competition in the NFC. Clearly it was going to be a cakewalk all the way to the Super Bowl. McNabb, Owens and company ran the team's record all the way to 13-1 before losing the last two games of the season, which were meaningless and hardly featured any of the Eagles' key players. It was time to rest up for the playoffs.

After a first round bye, the Eagles welcomed the Vikings to town. Minnesota was fresh off an upset win at Lambeau Field over the Packers. You remember the game. Randy Moss scored a touchdown and then fake-mooned the crowd, much to the disgust of Joe Buck. It was pretty funny. Thankfully, Moss would not get the chance to do the same in Philadelphia, as the Eagles triumphed 27-14 for a fourth straight NFC Championship Game appearance, this time against the Atlanta Falcons.

Well, this was it. No in between. Either the Eagles would win and finally make a long overdue Super Bowl appearance or they would lose and be a complete and utter failure, a minor league version of the Buffalo Bills team that lost four straight Super Bowls in the 1990's. On cue, a blanket of snow fell on Philadelphia the night before the game, providing a perfect landscape for either a magnificent conquest or catastrophic letdown.

Just like the Flyers in the previous spring, I was getting that "team of destiny" feeling about the Eagles. Would I be right this time? The first half against Atlanta was solid yet unspectacular, with the Eagles taking a precarious 14-10 lead into the break. But despite being too close for comfort, I never got a sense of impending doom. A couple David Akers field goals stretched the lead and it was 20-10 headed to the fourth quarter. Spirits were high, and so were a lot of the fans at Lincoln Financial Field I'm sure.

The scoring would conclude on McNabb's iconic toss into the corner of the endzone that was hauled in by Chad Lewis, who kept his feet just inbounds for the score. It was a snow-covered celebration for the players and fans alike. There was more white powder flying around than at a strip club hosting a party for the mid-90's Cowboys. This was actually happening. The Eagles won. The Eagles won. For the first time in my life, they were going to the Super Bowl. I knew it all along.

High on excitement (and nothing else), my friend Bill and I went out to Hooters for some reason to celebrate and watch some of the AFC Championship Game to see who the Eagles' opponent would be. We were both a few months shy of turning 21, so I guess we toasted the Birds with soda. I can't remember. But I do remember inconsiderately jumping into a huge snow bank in jubilation right before hopping into his car and then getting a ton of snow all over his seats despite my efforts to brush it off of me.

You'd better believe that the next two weeks on *Sports Talk Philadelphia* featured wall-to-wall Eagles coverage, first the analysis of their NFC title and then a look ahead to the Super Bowl, which would be against the New England Patriots after they had dispatched the Steelers for the AFC crown.

The matchup was, objectively, an extremely close one. I feared the worst but held out legitimate hope that this was finally it. I even went so far as to not pick a winner when we made our predictions on the show. I called a score of 23-17 with a big fat question mark in the winning column. My most notable contribution, however, leading up to the "big game" were my closing remarks on the show, which we taped three days prior to the Super Bowl. We had a segment called "Minute Madness", which was our label for the portion at the end of the program where a panelist got to talk uninterrupted. Sports shows just love to do these kinds of things, as I'm sure you probably know. Here is what I chose to say in my segment:

"Win together today and we walk together forever". Those words were scrawled on a blackboard by Flyers coach Fred Shero on May 19, 1974 to inspire his players, and they went out that night and they won, defeating the Boston Bruins 1-0 to win that Stanley Cup Final four games to two. And I bring this up because it reminds me a lot of the current situation. The Flyers were an underdog to a team from New England looking for their third title in five years, and the Eagles are underdog to a team from New England looking for their third title in four seasons this weekend. That was 11,221 days ago Sunday that Fred Shero wrote that message and the Flyers won. And that ushered in a golden age of Philadelphia sports with the Flyers winning the next year, making a few other finals appearances, Eagles making a Super Bowl, Phillies finally winning a World Series after 100 years in the basement…and the Sixers won on May 31, 1983 which, as of Sunday, was 7,922 days ago. So it's been a while and of course no city or area with as

many professional teams as we have has gone that long without a championship. We've had minor things along the way: the Phantoms won, the Philadelphia Barrage of course as I mentioned earlier this year, but we're looking big time here, people. No one wants or deserves a championship more than the long-suffering fans here in Philadelphia. So, to the Philadelphia Eagles this weekend, I say win together Sunday and Philadelphia fans everywhere will remember you forever.

Would my words echo down the corridors of history? Or would they simply be seen by a smattering of people and immediately be forgotten because of the result of the game only to be dredged back up in a book over a decade later? There was nothing left to do but to play the game and find out. PS Ignore the fact that I misquoted Fred Shero. The first "together" isn't part of the quote he wrote on the blackboard. But in the interest of accuracy, I've included it in the transcript. Still, you get the point.

The game began. Nothing in the first quarter. But then my hopes spiked in the immediate aftermath of McNabb's TD pass to LJ Smith to open the scoring in the second quarter. For one shining moment, it all seemed like the dream was going to come true. I could picture the crushing throng of Eagles nuts parading down Broad Street two days later. But when the Patriots tied it 7-7 just before halftime, that old familiar dread returned. In fact, the Eagles had had so many missed opportunities that it felt like they were behind rather than being deadlocked at the break. I knew that New England wouldn't sleep on them for long. The teams headed to the locker room, and out came Paul McCartney to perform at halftime. I maintain that because he sung for way way too long, the Patriots were able to make all the necessary adjustments they needed to during that interminable intermission. They probably also checked the spy tapes they had made but that none of us knew about yet.

So it came as no surprise to me when they took the ball at the start of the second half and marched right down the field for a score. More shocking to me was that the Eagles responded later in the quarter rather than just fading away, and so it was 14-14 after the third quarter, which was about all you could hope for. But the Patriots would rattle off ten points to start the fourth and then intercept McNabb to seemingly put the game away. The Eagles, to their credit, showed some life with a late TD, although it came at the expense of the clock during that infamous drive where they used a full huddle the entire time and took far too long. My favorite play was the 2-

yard swing pass to backup fullback Josh Parry that basically ate up a minute of game time. McCartney must have dialed that one up.

The Eagles failed to recover the onside kick, and the Patriots forced them into using all of their timeouts. When the Eagles got the ball back, it was with under a minute left and in the shadow of their own goalposts. It didn't end well, as you know and probably expected all along anyway. In the immediate aftermath of a game like that, your emotions are a mixed bag. Sadness and frustration. *They were so close!* Hope for the next year. *We'll be back!* Wanting to murder people. *Murder, murder, murder!*

The season was a great ride, no doubt, but it felt like the end to me. This wasn't a young team building up to a championship, it was a last hurrah. Missed chances in previous NFC Championship Games had taken their toll. The Eagles' teams of this era should have been in another Super Bowl or two, and once you're there anything can happen. Maybe a lucky bounce goes your way and you get a parade out of it. But it just wasn't meant to be. A win would have galvanized the fanbase and brought the franchise out of its decades-long punchline status. Instead, the wait continued.

As if all this weren't bad enough, I forgot to mention that the Flyers weren't even playing. The NHL's owners and players were still miles apart on a new CBA, and after hemming and hawing for months, had finally canceled the 2004-05 season. They couldn't even figure things out in time for a short slate of games, waiting too long to salvage anything at all. We had covered it in detail for months on *Sports Talk Philadelphia*, but we gave it little heed after they had officially canceled the season. If they didn't care enough to give the fans a product to watch, why should we bother spending any more time talking about it? I'd let them come to their senses and get back to me when they did.

Following the Super Bowl postmortem, we were basically forced to talk Sixers on our show for over a month until the Phillies got going. Though I had never followed them very closely, I was able to educate myself to a semi-knowledgeable level so that I could make salient points about the team and offer critical analysis of the way that they were playing. As a study in contrast, my friend and co-host Matt went for shock value, shooting from the hip and yelling a lot while still lamenting the lack of NHL to entertain him. This will end up playing a part later in my story.

And so the Phillies geared up for 2005 with a new manager at the helm. Lost in all of the Eagles excitement over the last few months was the fact that the club had parted ways with Larry Bowa after four seasons and hired veteran baseball man Charlie Manuel as their "next man up". But Uncle Charlie and his good ol' boy ways didn't seem to be much of a fit in this town to me. Upon his hiring, I was critical of it on the show. I had wanted Jim Leyland, who I had always liked going back to his tenure with the Pirates. Leyland had also won a World Series with the Marlins, so he had that advantage over Charlie as well.

But even more mind-boggling to me was that Ed Wade was STILL the GM. Not only should he have gone when Bowa did, his ouster was at least a couple years overdue already. The whole situation had the smell of something that was going to crash and burn relatively quickly and I felt like Manuel wasn't likely to last long. Francona and Bowa each got four years, so maybe that was the expiration date for Charlie as well. There were some promising young players on the team and waiting in the minors as well, but when did that stuff ever work for the Phillies?

A few weeks of average baseball into the season, we wrapped our last show of the spring semester and my junior year was over. Life was just happening too fast. I was really expected to be an adult with a steady job in just over twelve months? Most importantly, I was going to be a college senior without having seen a Philadelphia title in my lifetime. How much longer was this going to take?

*

5.

ENDINGS AND BEGINNINGS

All of a sudden, I was a college senior. After an eventful summer that included my girlfriend of 3+ years ostensibly breaking up with me, I came back to school feeling glum about that but nevertheless excited about my little sports show and perhaps getting a chance at an internship during the school year. The Philly sports landscape was, as usual, a hodgepodge.

The Sixers, unsurprisingly, had gone out meekly in the first round of the playoffs back in the spring. Of course the Flyers hadn't even gotten a chance to play their season at all, but at least the lockout was now over and the NHL was set to rise from its self-created ashes again in the fall. In the Flyers' absence, the Phantoms won the Calder Cup that year as they played to huge crowds at the Wachovia Center, trying to fill part of the void left in the hearts of people like me who were hungry for hockey. My dad and I attended the clinching game, and although it may be the only time I ever see a Philadelphia team win a championship in person, I don't remember a whole lot of it. I imagine my excitement was about 1% as much as it would be if the Flyers ever won, and all I could think of was how great it would be if these young players could take the next step and win it all for the big club at some point. As for the other teams, the Eagles were hoping to avoid the Super Bowl hangover, and the Phillies were actually in the mix as the baseball season careened toward its final month.

Ultimately those 2005 Phils would fall short in their quest to get back to the playoffs, and I point to one singular game as the culprit. On September 7 that season, I went to CBP to watch the Phillies take on the Astros, with whom they were neck and neck in the wild card chase. The game had a playoff feel and a real excitement to it that had been sorely lacking during almost all Phillies home games over the previous decade. Heading into that game, the Phillies were 0-5 so far that year against Houston and it would be the teams' final meeting.

With the Phillies clinging to a 6-5 lead entering the ninth inning, things looked pretty good as stud closer Billy Wagner came in and promptly retired the first two hitters he faced. But then a defensive gaff by David Bell at third base kept the Astros' hopes alive. Bell hadn't done much to endear himself to Philadelphia fans (me in particular) in his three seasons with the team, and this wasn't going to help his cause at all.

Wagner could still see his way out of things, but he allowed a hit to the next batter to put the go-ahead run on base. That's when Wagner's former long-time teammate Craig Biggio stepped up to the plate. The future Hall of Famer knew just what to look for and blasted a three-run home run to put the Astros up 8-6. Houston closer Brad Lidge (who would play an important role a couple years later) closed the door on the Phillies with ease in the bottom of the ninth to seal a season sweep for the visitors.

This truly ended up being the death knell for the Phillies' chances that season, even though they did play very well over its final 22 games, going 15-7. But you aren't doing yourself any favors by going 0-6 against your chief competition. In the end, the Phillies finished one game, a single misery-inducing game, behind Houston for the wild card. If Wagner could have only held the lead, if Bell didn't boot that ball, if they had won ANY of the other five games against Houston that year, the teams would have swapped records and the Phillies would have been in! Yes, this is big-time revisionist history, but it only serves to prove my point. Our team will always come up short in toss-up situations like that year's NL wild card race. To make matters worse, the Astros went all the way to the World Series that year. So close, yet so far.

One week after the Phillies' season came to an end, the team did manage to do something great. THEY FINALLY FIRED ED WADE! And on my 21st birthday, no less. I could not have asked for a greater present. When the guy wasn't busy picking up drinks that little kids had knocked over, he was making bad free agent signings and getting his pants pulled down by other GMs in trades. I was adamant that the team had to go outside of the organization for the new hire rather than simply promoting someone from within. Someone like, say, Ruben Amaro Jr. They'd just be spinning their wheels.

I was personally pulling for them to hire Gerry Hunsicker, who had been with the Astros for a decade and had put together several playoff teams over that span, as we had just seen firsthand. In the end, the Phillies chose veteran baseball mind Pat Gillick. It wasn't a bad move, just not my first preference. But it was definitely better than just going with the "keep it in the family" strategy that the organization had long been practicing. The Flyers are even worse with this kind of thing, but that's a whole other issue entirely. For the thousandth time I thought, "Maybe the Phillies are finally putting things together".

Also during that offseason, Ryan Howard had been named NL Rookie of the Year after admirably filling in for an injured Jim Thome. I actually thought that Willy Taveras of the Astros should have won it after playing a full season and acting as the leadoff hitter for an eventual league champion. But what do I know? I was happy that a Phillie had won something for once.

One team that definitely wasn't winning anything that year was the Eagles. Hopes were high around town that the Super Bowl near-miss was a sign that they could get back to an unprecedented fifth straight NFC title game and then repeat as conference champions. But we should have known from Week 1 that things just weren't going to work out.

Before the game even started, Eagles linebacker Jeremiah Trotter was ejected in a pre-game fight. The team followed that up with a pretty listless 14-10 loss in their seemingly annual season-opening Monday Night Football defeat. They did manage to reel off three wins in a row after that, but it proved to be fool's gold as they lost four of the next five, also suffering a slew of injuries along the way that completely derailed the team and made it no fun to discuss on *Sports Talk Philadelphia*.

The absolute low point of the year and the final closure for the team's "championship window" came during another Monday Night Football game when they were honoring the late Reggie White by retiring his number. The Eagles lost 42-0 to Seattle that night and there was no doubt that the season was dead, the core players' prime years were wasted and this thing was a lost cause for the next little while. Factor in Terrell Owens' shenanigans and his ouster from the team and it was a pretty entertaining year, but for all the wrong reasons.

As for the whole T.O. debacle, I am ashamed to say that I fell victim to the groupthink mentality that was pervading the area at the time. Owens was vilified as a clubhouse cancer and the reason that the Eagles weren't going anywhere. When Andy Reid suspended him for the season, the move was widely celebrated. But in hindsight, the whole thing was as dumb as dumb gets.

Owens was producing at an incredible rate and was really the only guy who was doing his job. Personality and locker room influence aside, you need your best players on the field to give you a chance to win games. They were 4-4 at the time he was kicked off the team, still in the mix, but they limped to a 2-6 mark over the final eight games, including that Seattle blowout. They wouldn't have won that particular game if they had Owens and Jesus as their wide receivers, but you still get the point. Owens didn't do himself any favors. But Andy Reid, the Eagles and Philadelphia fans really "did him dirty" on this one. He was perhaps the most talented player to ever suit up in an Eagles uniform, but it was all over in the blink of an eye.

The trainwreck of an Eagles' season gave us a lot of fodder for ridicule on our show, but after a while we had to turn our attention to the Sixers and Flyers. With Maurice Cheeks at the helm and Chris Webber starting his first full season on the team, the expectations for the Sixers were decent. Iverson put on his usual scoring display all year long, but ultimately there wasn't enough there to help him (or maybe there weren't enough shots to go around) and the team finished sub-.500 and out of the playoff picture. Another season where I was correct in not getting excited at all about basketball.

I was, however, extremely hyped up about the Flyers even back in the fall when the Eagles were beginning their ill-fated Super Bowl follow-up campaign. The main reason for excitement was that the Flyers had brought Peter Forsberg back to town, over a decade after he was dealt away in the Eric Lindros trade. When he was on the ice, he formed an electric combo with winger Simon Gagne, who finally seemed to be capitalizing on his potential with a career year. Hell, I could have scored 25 goals skating on a line with Forsberg. Also, I can barely skate.

My dad and I got to witness a quirky bit of NHL history on December 6 that season in a game between the Flyers and Calgary Flames. Fellow Finnish netminders Antero Niittymaki and Miikka Kiprusoff dueled to a 0-0 draw through regulation and overtime, sending the game into the shootout, which was new to the NHL that season. The Flyers would eventually get the win; we didn't know how awful they'd end up being in shootouts yet. And though it goes down as a 1-0 final score, that goal doesn't actually count against a goalies' goals against average since it wasn't during a timed portion of the game, meaning that Kiprusoff became the first goalie in league history to lose a game where he was credited with a shutout. I also think that he and Niittymaki set a league record for most combined double letters in goalies' names that night.

But the most notable game that I got to attend that season had come a few weeks before in a November tilt against the very crappy Penguins featuring Sidney Crosby, my first in-person look at the whiny teenager. During the game, Flyers defenseman Derian Hatcher popped him in the mouth and knocked out several of Sid's baby teeth. It was awesome. In today's NHL, it probably would have resulted in a lengthy suspension, but Hatcher got no penalty on the play despite Sid's petulant protestations. Did I mention it was awesome? Unfortunately though, Crosby managed to get loose on a breakaway in overtime and score the winning goal, his second of the game, to get the last laugh that night. I wish I could say that this was just a blip on the radar in the Flyers-Penguins rivalry, but we all know better. Talk about luck, Pittsburgh. We'll get into this more later.

Games like this aside, the Flyers put together a solid year thanks to superb play by Forsberg. But the problem with him, as always, was injuries. Though he was only 32 years old at this point, a multitude of chronic injuries kept taking turns popping up throughout the year. The end result was a 60-game season for Forsberg, though he did register 75 points during that time. He was healthy enough for the playoffs and did everything he could to put the team on his back, totaling eight points in six games. But those six games would be all that the Flyers could muster, losing to Buffalo in the first round.

One thing that Forsberg did succeed in a few months before the NHL playoffs was capturing a gold medal for his native Sweden during the Winter Olympics, held that year in Torino, Italy (or Turin, if you're an Italian from South Philly). And I should probably mention now that I could have gone to the Olympics but passed up the chance to do so. It was nobody's fault but my own, as a combination of factors undermined my ability and willingness to take part in an amazing experience.

I cannot recall exactly when, but it was probably the previous summer that La Salle announced that they were among a select group of schools that would be sending students to Italy for the Olympics to work for NBC in carrying out the monumental production that was taking place over there. But while everyone else was likely clamoring for the chance to go, I had to think it over for a while. This revelation had completely thrown me off, as I had never once heard any kind of rumblings or indication that such a thing might happen. Had that been the case, I would have approached my entire last few years of college differently.

My plan all along was to take part in an internship at a local media outlet in my final semester of school, the spring of 2006. With any luck, this would provide an immediate stepping stone into the Philadelphia TV or radio broadcasting scene for me. If this Olympics thing had been anywhere on the radar previously, I would have tried to pull off the local internship a semester or two earlier, freeing up the final one for Torino.

By the time La Salle's Olympics participation was announced, it was too late to get any kind of local internship lined up for the fall of 2005, and so I was faced with the decision of proceeding with my original plan or going for the Italy trip in the spring of 2006 and not doing any kind of Philadelphia internship at all. Going to Torino also had the drawback of missing almost half a semester's worth of programming on La Salle 56, the recordings of which I was relying on to put together a demo reel of my work. Plus, I really enjoyed producing the show on a weekly basis and then trying to be equal parts entertaining and informative while I was on the air. In the end, I stuck to my guns. I would stay local, be the "glue" to hold together the station as its senior member for a bit while a good chunk of my peers went off to Italy, and continue with the plan to set up an internship with one of the Philadelphia stations. I had largely chosen La Salle because of the Philadelphia market and would not miss the chance to get my foot in the door at one of them.

My personal life was also skewing my point of view at this time as well. I had an eye toward salvaging my relationship with my sort-of girlfriend at the time, and I thought that going away for weeks on end would be the final blow for it. I should have been able to foresee that it wasn't going to end well, as it was headed for its second and final dissolution about three months after I graduated, but it was all I had known at that point and didn't want to let it go so easily. The game of love prevents people from going to Italy. I should have that emblazoned on a coffee mug.

That spring semester, the final one of my college life, did go pretty smoothly despite my inner turmoil. I definitely had the qualifications to be chosen for Italy, of that I had no doubt, and so I second-guessed myself on more than one occasion. But I did take a certain level of pride in steering *Sports Talk Philadelphia* by myself for the time that my four closest compatriots on the show were off having fun (but apparently working hard as well) for NBC in Torino.

We had some younger guys step up as temporary fill-ins before they would take over the show full-time the next fall, and they all did fine. But I felt lost without my usual foils on the show and around campus in general, as our communication department was like its own little school where you would have classes and eat meals with a lot of the same people. Those times were what I cherished the most about my time in college, and I missed out on them for a good while. Should I have gone to Italy? Again, probably, but I didn't have a time machine for 30-year old me to go back and set 20-year old me straight on the matter and yell at him for wimping out on it. Oh well.

That semester, I did get to see the inner workings of a real-life honest-to-goodness golly-gee-willickers television station as a sports department intern at one of the locals. It was a sobering taste of adulthood and responsibility. The crux of the "work" was watching and recording whatever game that was on that night and logging a shot sheet so that the producer could quickly edit some highlights for the sports segment during that night's broadcast. I split time with another intern, with each of us taking three nights a week and both of us in on Sunday (me from about noon-5, her from about 5-10pm) to cover the excess of sports on that day of the week.

It was pretty unglamorous but it made me hopeful for working my way up in the world. However, because of the repetitive nature of it, there wasn't much chance to shine and differentiate myself, so I am afraid that their final impression of me was that I was average. I did get to do some editing later on in the internship and put together a decent video project about it for school, but again, I probably didn't blow anyone away. The anchors and producers were all nice enough to work with, yet they were likely so used to the faceless procession of interns that came through the door every few months that they weren't easily impressed.

On a handful of occasions, I got to go out on the road in the sports van with a cameraman for some electronic news gathering (ENG, for those of us in the biz). And because of the time of year, it was always for basketball. One time, we saw St. Joe's lose an NIT game on their home court, which made me happy because I hate St. Joe's and laugh every time they lose. Another night, we tried to get to a local high school championship game for the second half but because of traffic we arrived with literally seconds left on the clock, saw the game-winning shot, and that was it. Two plus hours in the van for about a 12-second video clip.

We also went to the Palestra and watched about five minutes of a Harvard-Penn game just to get two or three "highlights". That one must have been a really slow night. And on one of these occasions, the camera guy stopped his van in a parking lot a few blocks from the station on the way back, got out and met some guy in the shadows. So I am 99% sure that I got to witness my first drug deal. It was thrilling.

But of all these kooky adventures on the road, the one that is singed most into my brain was when we went to cover a 76ers-Rockets game. The plan all along was to get there late in the contest to grab some shots and then gather some postgame sound. And so I watched the last few minutes of an 87-81 Sixers loss and then stood about two feet away from Rockets' coach Jeff Van Gundy in the tunnel after the game as he gave an interview. I'm not sure if he had just gotten a new round of hair plugs because it looked like a child had been playing connect-the-dots on his head with a purple marker but hadn't gotten around to drawing the lines yet. I heard nothing that he said.

After this was a trip to the Rockets' locker room and the part that I will never forget. I had heard about the casualness with which players in various state of undress would give interviews to the media following games. But I was not prepared. Everywhere I turned, my vision was peppered with hanging genitalia and I could not make it stop. But I will be eternally grateful that Dikembe Mutombo, on Houston at the time, was at least wearing a towel. It was a regular-sized towel, though proportionately it looked like a washcloth (barely) covering his lower body. It was just enough. Thank God it was enough. I don't know why all of these basketball experiences didn't make me a bigger fan of the sport…

A short while later, the Olympics ended, my friends came back, and we settled in for the final handful of shows that we would have together before graduation time. Side note: my classmates did such a bang-up job that La Salle was never again invited to provide interns for NBC for any future Olympics. Nice job, guys.

Also around this time, the La Salle communication department managed to organize a panel discussion featuring several members of the local sports media, most notably Phillies' public address announcer Dan Baker. I was positively giddy after the discussion when I got to speak to him and tell him it had always been my dream to hear him announce my name as a Phillie. And so, with gusto, I got him to say "Now batting for the Phillies, catcher Kevin Lagowski!" And my life was complete.

Kevin Lagowski

In the last days of my college life, we arrived at the inevitable: our final show at La Salle 56. Now, all of us have been parts of clubs and groups throughout our lives, and so I'm not going to pretend that my situation was any more special than someone else's was to them. But I was genuinely sad that we couldn't do our "dumb little show" every week anymore. I would be staying in touch with a good many of the people I shared the experience with, but the common cause bringing us all together was coming to an end. We had covered a lot between the fall of 2004 and the spring of 2006, however it seemed like there was so much more left to be said. And so, with a heaping of nostalgia and an eye toward the future, I delivered my final Minute Madness in (mostly) verse form…

The Bambino's curse broken / A receiver outspoken

A Super Bowl trip / The next season, a dip

The Phils and their hirings / Which were preceded by firings

Howard the rookie / Tocchet the bookie

Ovechkins and Sidneys / And donated kidneys

Simon scores from Peter / And Barry Bonds is a cheater

The Tar Heels, the Gators / And all the Duke haters

The Winter Olympics / And A.I. up to his old tricks

A BCS title in Austin / And my SportsTalk Boston

Iguodala and his jams / And Andy Reid enjoys hams

The wild card chase / And the sight of John Chaney's face

The Eagles, the Flyers / The Sixers, the Phils

We're all hoping someday soon / For championship thrills

Please, please, please. Because as has been mentioned here on the show before, the overriding message of SportsTalk Philadelphia is "Please somebody win". And unlike Matt Juliano, I think that someone will win soon. Granted, not overly soon perhaps. But soon the in the grand scheme of things. We'll be here to enjoy it. It will be wonderful. It will be like touching the face of God.

And then I went on, thanking everybody. You get the idea. That was a lot of fun and I wanted to make sure I printed it verbatim even if some of it makes zero sense to the people reading it now. Unless you saw the show. Which you didn't. Anyway, in those closing remarks, I clung to a glimmer of hope that even a fan like myself who had never won anything had a reason for legitimate optimism in the near future. That, and I took a shot at my good buddy Matt for his eternal pessimism.

We closed our last show, the four graduating seniors, with all the huggy-feely crap you'd expect. And I must give credit to my friend Ben, who was adamant that the team to finally break through and grab the brass ring in Philadelphia would be the 2009 Phillies. Now, Ben wasn't exactly staring into a crystal ball, as he was just relying on the pattern of finals appearances that had happened in town over the last decade-plus: 1993 Phillies, 1997 Flyers, 2001 Sixers, 2005 Eagles (2004 season, Super Bowl in 2005). So by his reasoning, it was the Phillies' turn in 2009. Wait, now I'm confused. Was he saying the Phillies would just make the World Series, not win it? That's a bummer. Anyway, spoiler alert: Ben nailed it, at least in terms of a Philly team losing in the final of their sport in 2009. But something else notable did occur between the time of his proclamation and 2009 that I may have time to get to in this book…

Like a flash, college was done. Real world time. Would sports even continue to enjoy a prominent position in my life now that "fun and games" time was officially over? In my quest to slide in on the ground floor of my chosen field, I applied for an open production assistant job at the station where I had just been interning for the past four months. This seemed like an ideal situation for me. Yeah, it didn't pay that much and it was a long commute from Delaware to the city, but I would make it work and had other part-time prospects on the table that could supplement my income. And so I got my first taste of rejection in the industry when I received a cold, informal postcard in the mail from said station that simply said something along the lines of "We have chosen another candidate to fill the open position. Thank you for your interest, and please continue to monitor our website for future" blah blah blah.

Obviously, I had prominently featured my internship on the resume that I had submitted for the job. And so I thought that my candidacy was worth at least a phone call or further exploration by whoever was doing the hiring. I think for a brief time I even had myself convinced that the job was a done deal. But this was a sobering moment that showed me that things weren't going to just be handed to me. Also, that station could take their damn job and shove it. I didn't need them.

Out of the blue, a short while after graduation, I got a phone call from the programming director at WPEN (950 AM) in Philadelphia. The station had recently switched to an all-sports format and was looking to compete with incumbent juggernaut WIP. Apparently he had seen our final episode on La Salle 56 and liked what he saw from me, specifically my aforementioned Minute Madness with the poem and the plea for a winning team. See, there was a reason I included it here. He also was intrigued by my friend Matt and the way he always seemed mad about everything. In his mind, we were good candidates to have our own show together.

I was floored. It couldn't really be that easy, could it? I had been out of college for mere weeks and here was the programming director of a top-market station wanting to put me on the air. Even better, it would be an afternoon-drive slot and I'd get to do it with one of my friends. Of course, I presumed there would have to be some kind of interview process and an air check. But since he was the once who reached out to us, it was a great sign that we might be spouting our opinions to the masses in the very near future.

Matt and I quickly convened to come up with some ideas and waited to hear back from the guy (his name long since forgotten by me) for our next move. We figured we would hear back in a week or two so he could meet us and discuss his view for a potential show. Instead, time dragged on and we heard nothing. Then we got anxious and tried contacting him ourselves, to no avail. Finally, Matt got wind that he had already left the station. Great. Was he just throwing crazy ideas at the wall and his last order of business before he went out the door was to get a couple guys' hopes up for no good reason? Anyhow, we did eventually get a hold of his replacement, who promptly blew us off in the most polite way possible. The Philadelphia sports landscape was finding new and exciting ways to screw me over beyond the teams just stinking.

After this experience, if you can call it that, I didn't know what to think. Did I almost have a job in Philly sports radio right out of school, or was this all some kind of mistake or cruel joke? One positive from all of this is that Matt and I went from being acquaintances bordering on friends to being very good friends from that point forward, enjoying shared interests (mostly sports) together for years to come and eventually being groomsmen at each other's weddings. The experience brought us together and galvanized us in some strange way. So I guess 950 was good for something at least, as they plodded along for a few years before shedding their sports format. Maybe it would have been different if they had hired me. In fact, I'm confident that they would have overtaken WIP. You can't prove otherwise.

As I continued to work assorted jobs after college, including one at a funeral home, I was able to catch on with the ArenaVision crew at the then Wachovia Center with the help of a friend. Sometimes it's just who you know and/or being in the right place at the right time. I was excited because I was going to get paid to watch sporting events. You know, while I worked at them. So there was that part of it. But I was getting paid to go to games! This was a big deal for me. And so, beginning with the 2006-07 season, I got to ply my craft (but mostly just get paid to watch sports) for ArenaVision a few times a month as I juggled that job with several other part-time positions. Man, I was busy then. I even had to resort to writing everything on a piece of paper that I jammed into my wallet so I could keep my different shifts straight on a daily basis. Remember when we didn't have smartphones?

I knew the work at ArenaVision wasn't going be glamorous, and I got the full rundown during an orientation. I was one of several "AV tech" guys that would pair up with a camera operator during a game and more or less "pull their cable" while I followed them around for that night's event. Believe me, I have been playfully mocked by several coworkers for my time spent as a "cable puller" ever since. So just as the Phillies were wrapping up another non-playoff season despite the MVP exploits of Ryan Howard (58 home runs!), I began my time as an employee in the world of Philadelphia sports. Kinda sorta.

Of course, I was most excited about working Flyers games and would put up with basketball and the rest of it when I had to. Again, at least they would be paying me to be there and not the other way around. As it was, hockey games were the easiest ones to work and gave me the most chance to watch the action. Most of my work was done before the game, as I lugged a heavy handheld camera and its accompanying 100-foot cable all around the building to three or four drop boxes to "fax out" and make sure the connections were all good to go. Theoretically, all of this stuff should have been fine since the last time it was used, but I guess my cheap labor was worth ensuring that nothing was wrong.

My travels around the building would frequently take me into the bowels of it, down behind the team's locker rooms. There I would often see hockey players huddled into groups kicking a soccer ball around before their pre-game skate, a favorite activity of many, especially European-born players who grew up playing both sports. As I ambled along once before a Flyers-Capitals game, Alex Ovechkin sent a ball flying about a foot past my head and down the hallway. Had I been quicker to react, I could have leaned out in front of it and gotten to meet him after taking it in the face, maybe even getting a pity autograph out of it in the process.

After walking all over the whole building, I still had enough time for a free pre-game meal, which was a nice perk of the job, before going off with the camera guy (or gal) to either the Zamboni tunnel for the national anthem or some other assigned section for the first period. If we were designated to cover the anthem, we had to hustle after it was over to get to our next section before the first television timeout. But the movements for the rest of the game were free and easy. We'd just sit or stand there and watch the play, and then shoot the crowd during stoppages and commercial breaks. Then, we'd move to our next section at the first intermission and our final assigned spot during the second intermission. After the game, there was nothing to clean up, so I could just take the equipment back upstairs and was good to leave. The lion's share of the work was done early in the night, I got the free meal and then was able to watch almost all of the game. A great deal all around.

Up until this point of my life, I had been going to about eight or ten Flyers games per year with my dad. He shared a season ticket plan with one of his friends, and I was spoiled by being able to go to virtually every game that I had my eye on. I played a game of "collect them all" and made sure that I saw every other team in the league at least once over the years. Call me a completist. Because I am. Now, between the games I was attending "as a fan" plus the ones I would be working, I ended up at over half of the Flyers' home games that first season working in the building. So it was just my luck that the Flyers were the absolute worst team in the league that year by a huge margin. Of the 21 games I was at, they won only six of them. And they lost the first EIGHT games that I worked. I never thought that I would dread going to a Flyers game that I would be getting paid to be at, but by the end of that year, it happened.

Aside from the team sucking, the experience was enjoyable. And I may or may not have used my employee parking pass for some of the games I attended as a fan. One thrill for me was working with Stephenie LaGrossa of *Survivor*, a show that I was a big fan of at that point. That year, Stephenie happened to be doing in-arena work for Flyers games, so this put me in close proximity to her on occasion. She was very nice but probably thought I was a total creep when I asked her to pose for a picture so I could send it to my friend, who was also a *Survivor* watcher. In the pre-selfie age, it was all I could think of to document that I had met her. It was one of my first brushes with a famous person, depending on how you define famous, and I had no idea how to act. Forgive me for my ignorance.

Every other event at ArenaVision was far less enjoyable and entailed more work than Flyers games. 76ers games, of course, made up most of the other gigs, and I worked a lot of them. The "process" (foreshadowing?) for Sixers games was the exact inverse of how things went for the Flyers. Before the game, all I had to do was take the camera and cable down to the floor and plug into one drop. As long as everything checked out, I was free to go and eat. But the game itself, starting with the warmup before it, was an endless nightmare of shuttling on and off the court for the entire night. Every single timeout, of which there are quite a few during NBA games, we'd have to weave our way between a ton of obstacles just to go and shoot the cheerleaders for twenty or thirty seconds. Lather, rinse, repeat. My cable would become a tangled mess that I'd be fooling with all night, and caused major issues for me on more than one occasion. Pulling your cable all night isn't all it's cracked up to be.

One night during warmups I attempted to run the cable perfectly down the baseline and around the corner so my cameraman could shoot a courtside interview, but I guess it flapped out on the court by a couple inches, much to the chagrin of the Lakers' Derek Fisher, who yelled at me. "Man, get that rope out the way!" Maybe I would have made headlines if he had fallen and gotten hurt. At least it wasn't as bad as the time my cameraman was shooting the Sixers' dancers' halftime routine and for some reason decided to weave his way up the row and between several of them while they moved in every direction. Perhaps this would have been fine with a wireless camera, but for the poor sap holding his cable, it was a near-death experience as I dodged flying legs and angry glares from beautiful girls.

During another warmup, a woman holding a toddler on her lap was on ArenaVision for some reason when an errant rebound bounced over and bopped the kid directly in the face. The child's delayed and then hysterical reaction was simultaneously heart-breaking and funny. Don't worry though, the little guy was ok. I think. All this aside, you definitely had to earn your money working Sixers games. It's probably a good thing I'm not overly partial to basketball because you saw very little of the action when you worked the games. Plus, the Sixers had their usual sub-.500 season and weren't much fun anyway.

Finally, the absolute worst part was the postgame breakdown. Someone had the brilliant idea that poor bums like me would be responsible for climbing under the scorer's desk, with broadcasters still sitting there doing postgame wrap-up, and yanking out all of the cables we needed so they could be coiled up and put on a cart for the next time. Unlike Flyers games where your work was essentially done when the final horn sounded, this part took me and two other people no less than twenty minutes to complete every time. And games always seemed to have a way of going to overtime just to make you stay there even longer. I rooted for blowouts one way or the other so they could just get it over with and teams wouldn't keep fouling to stop the clock down the stretch. The work overall was about five times as much as it was for a Flyers game, and for me it was 1/100th as fun.

Along with the two main teams, other events I worked included Villanova basketball, the Soul (arena football) and the Wings (indoor lacrosse). The 'Nova games weren't as much work as the Sixers' games and at least they were shorter. The Soul and Wings games weren't very busy either, but I had no idea how long those sports dragged on and on until I was actually there in person. Good Lord, arena football is brutal. I did get to share an elevator with Mike and Mike (Greenberg and Golic) before one game, however, and did the appropriate butt-kissing. Don't judge me.

Somehow during all this, I managed to plan a 9-day trip to Spain with Bill for the first few days of 2007. Our travels did include the debauchery you would expect, but we also crammed a good deal of history and culture in, as Bill was in the process of achieving his master's degree in Spanish. Just as significantly, the Eagles had rebounded that season to post a 10-6 record and win the NFC East, setting up a first round playoff matchup with the Giants. It was going to be epic, but we were across the ocean for it. And let me remind you that even though 2007 doesn't seem that long ago, it was the stone age of technology as compared to today. We couldn't just pop into a bar to watch American football either. We had hit up a local internet café a couple times during our trip to stay connected to life back home, and so we decided that going back there would be our only shot to watch the game.

Thanks to the time difference, the Sunday afternoon start in Philadelphia meant that it was already a dark and desolate January evening in Madrid as we settled in to watch the game after paying some kind of fee on the NFL's website to get video access. I made sure to stay completely focused on the small computer screen with less than ideal sharpness, partly because of the intensity of the playoff game but mostly because of what was going on around us.

Porn. Lots and lots of porn. Just porn everywhere. A bunch of dudes watching porn. That's what internet cafes were for! We didn't know this ahead of time. I had a guy breathing heavily three feet to my right watching porn. People behind me that I mercifully couldn't see were definitely watching porn too. I guess it was just an understood thing without having to hang a neon "PORN" sign out front. Was it like this elsewhere in Europe and America? I'm assuming that smartphones have wiped out this practice, and I'm not sure if places like that even exist anymore. Anyway…

It was a tight contest as the Eagles and Giants slugged it out. The Eagles took a 20-10 lead into the fourth only to see it evaporate with a few minutes left. But Jeff Garcia and the Eagles would not be denied, getting the ball into field goal range to set up David Akers' winning kick at the buzzer. We erupted in triumph, probably not the only guys to do so at the internet café that night. As we danced into the street, we were pumped up and wanted to chase the feeling by going out and partying. But downtown Madrid at 10:30 on a Sunday night in January was pretty damn dead. So it was back to our crappy little hostel. We might have had an Amstel Light left in the fridge.

The Eagles' season would end the next week. I watched back on home turf as they played tough but were beaten by the Saints. It was a rare case of a Philadelphia team outperforming their talent and the fans' expectations. These kinds of things were nice and all, but this was getting serious. We were at the 24-year mark since the town's last title and Philly fans everywhere were dying for a winner. Like we said on *SportsTalk Philadelphia*, somebody please just win. We couldn't afford to be picky at this point. Would anyone finally step up?

*

Kevin Lagowski

6.

WE ACTUALLY WON

Just as the Flyers were in the death throes of that miserable 2006-07 season, the Phillies once again got back to work, their eyes set on the postseason after twelve consecutive years out of it, which doesn't include the 1994 season when baseball decided to ruin itself. Inexplicably, however, shortstop Jimmy Rollins made an offseason proclamation that the Phillies were "the team to beat in the NL East". Rollins' swagger had long been viewed as a positive by the fans, but this seemed excessive. The Phillies were a team on the rise, but they had finished a dozen games back of the Mets the previous year and it didn't seem like they would be leapfrogging them too soon.

Any hopes the Phillies had of sneaking up on people in 2007 were gone the moment Rollins decided to provide bulletin board material for the Mets and really the league as a whole. This guy had never won a thing in the big leagues but had the gall to say something like this. How dare he? It certainly seemed like it was going to be a foot-in-mouth situation that would go down in infamy like so many other moments in Philadelphia sports history.

The Phillies struggled right out of the gate and Rollins got roasted. Somewhere in the midst of their 4-10 start, I changed at least one of my fantasy baseball team's names to "The Team to Beat". And even though we hadn't made it out of April yet, the season felt DOA. The strides made in the previous years and the anticipation of something special was hanging by a thread already. But the Phillies managed to pull themselves up over .500 by the time summer hit. Maybe they had a chance after all.

In a moment of ignominy, they collected the franchise's 10,000[th] loss on July 15th of that year. The national media of course had to make light of how much the Phillies suck, largely glossing over the fact that they are the oldest team playing in the oldest league, which also has twice as many games per season as any other sport. Yeah, they're not the Yankees, but give me a break. The game was on ESPN, the Worldwide Leader in Ruining Sports. God forbid they air anything besides Yankees-Red Sox most of the time, but they just had to stop by for this "historical" moment. When the Phillies were subpar-to-bad for most of the previous decade, their existence was barely acknowledged nationally. But ESPN is great at making something out of nothing and made sure to be there for this glorious occasion, regardless of the simple law of averages that dictates some team would be the first one to get to a certain number of losses at some point. Wow, what a nice round number of losses, let's make a big deal out of it. Thanks.

With all that crap over with, the Phillies were within two games of the Mets as September rolled around. This was it. Would they fold under pressure or could Rollins' prophecy come true? Nobody was thinking World Series, as just a mere trip to the postseason would be a monumental accomplishment and thrill the city when it really needed a jolt from one its teams. Oh right, we always need that.

But the excitement quickly fizzled as the Mets got hot, the Phillies slipped, and the two-game gap widened to seven by September 12. That had to be it, right? The Phillies would never be able to overcome such a deficit. This was the franchise ridiculed the world over for their collapse in 1964, and it would take a similar situation for the proverbial shoe-on-the-other-foot scenario to occur in 2007. The Mets were a veteran team built to win and had made the NLCS the previous year, the Phillies not so much. It would be absolutely improbable for a comeback to happen.

But that's why they play the games, folks. Things started to get interesting as that extreme seesaw of a season reached the home stretch. The teams faced off at Shea Stadium, with the Mets having an opportunity to bury the Phillies for good. But the Phils were able to pull off a three-game sweep and cause the Mets faithful to start sweating even more than their morbid obesity usually caused on its own. The Phillies had beaten the Mets in the teams' final eight meetings that season. I guess they really were the team to beat in the NL East after all.

By September 27, the Phillies had wiped away the entire deficit and pulled even in the divisional race. The top of the National League that year was a big logjam of teams, so this was not a case where falling short would still mean a wild card berth. No, it was the division or bust. On September 28, I was among the throngs filling Citizens Bank Park to capacity as they beat the Nationals 6-0. Coupled with a Mets loss that night, the Phillies took sole possession of the division lead for the first time all year. I think I breakdanced out of the game. This was so damn exciting. They were going to do it. The next day brought a blip on the radar. The Mets won and the Phillies lost, so the teams were even again. One game left.

With the possibility of a one-game playoff looming if the teams either both won or both lost on that final day, that air of uncertainty crept back into my heart and mind again. Did they really come all the way back just to let it slip away on the season's final day? Or even worse, were they going to lose the one-game playoff in some grand fashion that would never be lived down in this city? You'll have to forgive me for seemingly flip-flopping every game. I really did believe in the team, I just wanted to guard against the pain and be prepared for a massive hurting so that it wouldn't completely crush my soul when it inevitably came.

That day's Mets/Marlins game was to start half an hour before the Phillies and Nationals had their first pitch. This presented an interesting situation for the Phillies and us fans, who could closely monitor that game and react accordingly. Would it be "win and you're in" or just "don't lose or you're out"? The Mets game would probably only be in the second inning by the time Jamie Moyer took the mound that day, so chances are that nothing too dramatic would transpire before the Phils game got underway. But then an amazing thing happened.

Tom Glavine, the same guy who had spurned the Phillies and signed a free agent contract with the Mets, was immediately destroyed by the Marlins' offense in the top of the first inning. He recorded a single out before being chased from the game, his last one as a Met, and it was 7-0 Marlins by the time the Phillies' game started. The fans were delirious. This final game that had a pall of doubt cast over it just a little while ago all of a sudden became a raucous party. Never mind that the Phillies still had to win; the Mets had totally fallen apart and the division was ours for the taking. This was no doubt going to be a clinching game, and you could book the trip to the playoffs. The sight of Mets' players and fans hanging their heads in disbelief made it all the sweeter. For the love of God, Phillies, please take care of business today.

Despite decades of Phillies baseball that would lead you to believe otherwise, the team did indeed go out and beat Washington that day, scoring in the first inning and never relinquishing the lead en route to a 6-1 victory, the NL East title and the team's first playoff appearance this century. The celebration was underway well before Brett Myers froze the Nationals' Wily Mo Pena's sorry ass for the final out and tossed his glove skyward in jubilation, but now it was official. The Phillies had overcome a 7-game deficit over the season's final 17 games to snatch victory from the Mets. It was a collapse of epic proportions for New York, and it was just about the most satisfying thing that ever happened around here.

Jimmy Rollins, he of the "team to beat" proclamation that had gotten under everyone's skin, had put together a stellar season with 30 home runs, 94 RBI and 41 stolen bases. He played in every game and set a new single-season major league record by coming to the plate 778 times, eclipsing the mark of 773 previously set by Lenny Dykstra for the 1993 Phils. The man simply showed up to play, got the job done and was later named MVP for his efforts. This was the obvious turning point from him being a "nice player" to Phillies' fans realizing how lucky they were to have him.

But even with the merriment ignited by the division win (and thrill of being able to laugh at the Mets), focus had to be shifted onto the playoffs. The Phillies drew the Colorado Rockies, who were absolutely on fire after winning 14 of their last 15 to end the regular season, including a one-game playoff against San Diego. At this point, the Phillies were playing with house money and everyone was in the classic "just happy to be there" mindset, but it was pretty disappointing when Colorado took each of the first two games in Philadelphia and then put the Phillies meekly to bed once the series shifted back to Denver.

In the blink of an eye, this dream season that put the team back on the map was over. Never mind that Rockies' closer Manny Corpas, who saved all three games, was clearly cheating by pouring soda all over his jersey and giving himself an illegal substance to rub onto the ball. That's cool, MLB, no need to do anything about that. Nothing to see there. Whatever. A sucky end to a season that deserved a better fate. And honestly, I got to see very little of the abbreviated playoff run because of my work schedule at the time. And so, the question became…Was this just lightning in a bottle, or could the Phillies build on 2007 and take the next step? We spent the whole offseason wondering and waiting.

Along the way, the Phillies made some minor moves to strengthen their depth, bringing in the likes of Geoff Jenkins and So Taguchi. They also signed Pedro Feliz to be their everyday third baseman. But the biggest transaction by far came courtesy of our old pal Ed Wade, at this point the GM for the Astros. He gifted closer Brad Lidge upon the Phillies, which both strengthened the Phils' bullpen and allowed Brett Myers to transition back to a starter, thereby seemingly bolstering the rotation as well. Things were coming together. And actually, Lidge was only the Phillies' second most important acquisition that offseason, as I weaseled my way into some freelance work at the ballpark for PhanaVision. Coupled with my ongoing work at the Wells Fargo Center, I was fully immersed in the Philly sports scene at that point. Jealous much?

The season started with a lot of promise, as the team actually managed to be over .500 by the end of April. This never happens for the Phillies. Every season you just assume they will start 5-12 and pretty much have one foot in the grave, racking up more losing series at that time of year than I do meatless Fridays. That's a Lent joke, in case you don't get it. The Phillies also had the city there for the taking at this point, with the Eagles having just finished an 8-8 season that was in no way fun or memorable.

In one of the first games I worked at the ballpark, I am pretty sure that I sealed my fate as persona non grata at PhanaVision by nearly getting into a fight with someone else in the control room, all because of the intricacies of the baseball save rule. There was some schlubby guy sitting over in the corner who I recall wasn't directly a member of the PhanaVision crew but rather worked for some other outfit that tracked stats or something. Obviously I wasn't paying attention when I was introduced. But this guy was there every game, so everyone knew him.

On the night in question, April 29, the Phillies were leading the Padres 7-2 after eight innings on their way to an easy win. With no need to use Brad Lidge in the ninth, Ryan Madson came in to finish it off. After getting two outs, he allowed a two-run home run, making the score 7-4. At this point, schlubby guy (I don't even remember his name, as you can tell) remarked that "At least Madson can get a save now". I immediately wanted to strangle this dude.

As you are probably aware if you are a baseball fan, the typical save situation (there are exceptions that I won't get into here) requires a team to have a lead of three runs or fewer. Yes, it was now 7-4 at this point in the game, but the three-run rule is contingent upon the pitcher throwing a full inning with said lead, not just recording one out like Madson still had to do after giving up the home run. And even more importantly, YOU CAN'T CREATE YOUR OWN SAVE SITUATION BY ALLOWING RUNS THAT THEN CUT YOUR TEAM'S LEAD DOWN TO THE SAVE THRESHOLD!

Schlubby guy was so wrong it hurt my brain to have to say anything to him, but I politely responded that Madson would not be getting a save for this game. But he stuck to his guns, necessitating me going further into detail about why he was wrong, yet he resisted. I stopped short of calling him a stone cold moron, but not by much. I truly feel that this encounter, which a bunch of people witnessed, basically ended any chance I had of sticking with PhanaVision long term. I worked only a handful of games the rest of the year, which was partly due to my gaining full-time employment elsewhere, thus putting a major dent into my freelance availability. But I'm sure they did not make it a priority to put me on the schedule.

I never worked at the ballpark again after 2008 although I did stay "on the roster" for the next two years, so I was issued an employee parking pass. That thing probably saved me, my dad and some friends a few hundred dollars for games we attended over those years. Guess I got the last laugh. Take that. Also, if you look up the Phillies-Padres box score for April 29, 2008, you'll get a definitive answer about who was right and understands the save rule. Sorry, schlubby guy.

But before we got too deep into the 2008 Phillies season, the "spring teams" of course had to settle up. The Sixers were average but made the playoffs because that's how the NBA rolls. Then they actually gave the Pistons a run for their money in the first round after splitting the first two games on the road and winning Game 3 in front of a rowdy home crowd in blowout fashion. I was there working that night and I have to say it was legitimately exciting. But the team failed to build on any momentum and lost three in a row to go quietly into that gentle night. The Flyers would have considerably more success.

A year after being easily the worst team in the NHL, the Flyers rebounded in a big way. They had had a typical Flyers offseason by bringing in guys like Scott Hartnell, Kimmo Timonen and Danny Briere. The moves worked for the most part as the Flyers got off to a good start (another thing that never happens) and then endured some late season struggles to squeak into the playoffs. They were a fun team to watch too, scoring the sixth most goals in the league that year and being the second most penalized team. Old time hockey, just how we like it.

Ron Hextall was inducted into the Flyers Hall of Fame in February of that season, and I was down at ice level for the ceremony, holding my cable as usual. In fact, I was so close that I overheard Flyers' GM Paul Holmgren being told to put his hand over the face of the bust he was presenting to Hextall because it was actually a bust of Dave Poulin, who at that point was the most recent Flyers Hall of Fame inductee. I guess their statue guy fell behind on his work and didn't have Hextall's ready on time, so they had to fudge it by re-using Poulin's for the ceremony. I'm also assuming that Holmgren had given said statue guy a new contract before that season since personnel mistakes were Holmgren's forte.

I also got to witness in person what were unquestionably the two greatest highlights of the brief NHL career of Flyers enforcer Riley Cote. First, he scored his lone NHL goal (in 156 games) with 19 seconds remaining in a 5-3 loss to Montreal. He really picked his spot on that one. Then, a scant 18 days later, he cemented his place in Flyers' lore with a one-punch KO of Tampa Bay thug Andre Roy in their second fight of the game. It was nothing short of awesome, and I was proud that ArenaVision milked it for all that it was worth by showing the replay no less than a dozen times, with the crowd whipping itself into a frenzy upon each viewing. In fact, the NHL actually changed its in-arena replay rules in the wake of this game to limit the number of times something could be shown. I guess they don't like when fans have fun and enjoy their product.

Making things even better, you could tell that Roy was enraged and embarrassed by both the knockout itself and the crowd's mockery of him because he had to be restrained on the Tampa bench after serving the penalty. He wanted another shot at Cote and was flying off the handle, only igniting the crowd further. It would be Roy's last appearance in a Lightning uniform, as he was benched for the rest of the game and made a healthy scratch for the remainder of the season, signing elsewhere over the summer. Cote even got third star honors for his effort in the game. What a middle finger to Roy. Everyone loved it.

But the most satisfying game that season for me had occurred back on December 11 on a night that I was working for ArenaVision. The Flyers obliterated the Penguins 8-2, with Joffrey Lupul and R.J. Umberger both recording hat tricks. I happened to be in the lower bowl during the third period and was able to hoist some of the hats that had fallen short over the glass, the first time in my life that I was able to land one directly onto the ice. Yeah, none of the hats were mine, but I'm counting it. I do, however, still have a bone to pick about that game to this day. Sidney Crosby was named third star for his two assists on the Penguins' goals, while Umberger wasn't even given one of the three stars. Clearly whatever moron picked the stars that night had mailed it in even more than the Penguins had. Maybe it was schlubby guy?

In the first round, the Flyers met the Washington Capitals. The Flyers actually had one more point during the regular season than the Caps but Washington had won their crappy division, so they had home ice. After dropping the opener, the Flyers then took three in a row, the last of which came on a double-overtime winner by Mike Knuble. But they failed in their first two opportunities to close the series out and so they were forced to go back to DC for a deciding seventh game. This was not good. After heartbreaking Game 7 losses in the '00 (Devils) and '04 (Lightning) conference finals, maybe this was going to hurt less by being earlier in the playoffs. I was prepared for the worst, as usual, but I failed to take note that the Flyers were facing the Capitals, one of the chokiest sports franchises around not named Mets. They would fix the issue a decade later, but we'll overlook that point right now.

In Game 7, as I was wearing my fingernails down to the nubs, the teams traded goals in each of the first two periods. Following a scoreless third, it was every hockey fan's subsequent dream and nightmare. Overtime. Visions of Jean-Claude Van Damme's classic film *Sudden Death* danced in my head, although this game probably wasn't going to end with a terrorist plummeting iceward to his death in a helicopter. Even if this didn't happen, I would still be happy with a simple Game 7 overtime win, something that had never taken place in Flyers history. And after the Flyers amazingly got a power play in said overtime, Joffrey Lupul poked in a loose puck to give them the win, send the Lagowski household into delirium and the Caps and their fans into a decade-long spiral of crushing playoff disappointments. It was wondrous, and I didn't honestly think at that moment that anything else in 2008 could top it.

The Flyers moved on to face the top-seeded Canadiens, and nobody was giving them a shot. They showed why by pissing away a pair of leads in a Game 1 overtime loss. But suddenly R.J. Umberger did his best Keith Primeau impression, the Flyers turned it on, and after four straight victories they were incredibly in the Eastern Conference Final, one season after being an unwatchable mess. They would meet the Penguins, and that was where the fun ended. Down 3-0 in the series, I went to Game 4 and was heartened that they didn't roll over and die, taking a 4-2 decision in that contest.

But that was all she wrote, as the Pens crushed them in Game 5 to head to the Cup Final. Thankfully they lost to Detroit, so I didn't end up feeling all too bad. In the end, it was the kind of season that reminded you how being a sports fan can be fun even if your team doesn't win it all. The team was entertaining all year and reached a level which everyone could be proud of. But as I slipped into full Phillies mode, I had to ratchet up my expectations. The Flyers' run was enjoyable, but this baseball club needed to take it to the next level for me to be satisfied. We now join the 2008 Phillies, already in progress.

Their season followed much the same script as 2007, with a late Mets swoon opening the door for the Phillies to take the division on the season's final weekend. Nothing could have been as satisfying as the way the previous season's comeback played out, but this was pretty good in its own right. Again the team would find itself facing the Nationals to end the regular season when, in the penultimate game, Jimmy Rollins started a nifty double play to seal the victory and clinch the division. As an added wrinkle, it also gave closer Brad Lidge his 41st and final save on the season to maintain his perfect record in that department. Even ol' schlubby guy at PhanaVision understood that one.

The final double play of Rollins to Utley to Howard was a seminal moment, not only because it featured the team's three most important offensive players of the era, but because of Tim McCarver's legendary call that went along with it. Working the game for Fox, McCarver was left alone in the broadcast booth for the ninth inning for some reason and capped the double play by exclaiming "The Phillies are National League division champions…of the East"! I must have rewound that one about ten times. To make things even sweeter, the Mets lost out on the wild card by a game, and so the Phillies would be taking on the Brewers in the first round of the playoffs.

Seeing as how I hadn't attended a playoff game in fifteen years, I figured I would bite the bullet and buy some tickets so my dad and I could go. I couldn't make Game 1, so Game 2 it was. The Phils took the opener and I was pretty much out-of-my-mind excited for the next one. Brett Myers was taking the mound for us, but standing in the way was Brewers' pitcher CC Sabathia. Sabathia had come over to Milwaukee at the trade deadline and had been nearly unbeatable. But in a frantic effort just to qualify for the playoffs, the Brewers had absolutely run him into the ground down the stretch, so maybe he was ripe for the picking at this point.

Game 2 started off poorly, with the Brewers scoring a run in the top of the first, but Myers worked himself out of a potential disaster by inducing a double play to end the inning. The Phillies tied it in the bottom of the second, and Myers came up to bat. His plate appearance would become the greatest walk in Phillies history. Yes, the greatest walk. Myers managed to foul a few pitches off of Sabathia as the crowd got louder and more boisterous. It was unbelievable. The stadium was rocking over a pitcher just barely getting enough bat on the ball to foul it off! Sabathia was obviously flustered and already looked like he was starting to tire. He was making his fourth straight start on short rest and had thrown a plethora of pitches over the last few months. Also, he was fat.

After nine pitches, Myers would eventually reach on a walk and the stadium was erupting. Rollins was up next and walked on four pitches. If ever a crowd completely got inside a pitcher's head, this was it. The Phillies needed to take advantage, and it was up to Shane Victorino to make it happen. Down 1-2 in the count, he turned on a high off-speed pitch and deposited it into the left field stands for the first grand slam in Phillies postseason history. I thought the building was going to fall down.

It is moments like these that make being a sports fan worthwhile. All the time, all the money, all the heartache. You freeze your butt off on a Tuesday night in April at the Vet when you're a kid, just sitting there with your dad watching a bad team and dreaming dreams that may never come. You hope that someday they will come, but you don't know for certain if they will ever materialize. And then something like this happens and you get to see it. I'm getting so misty-eyed I don't even think I can finish this paragraph. Wait, I made it.

Anyway, the Phillies would go on to win that game 5-2. Shifting back to Milwaukee, they lost Game 3, so it was time for the jitters again. But they would win Game 4 to polish off the series, which is a good thing because they would have had to face Sabathia again in the deciding game, and that would have been really pushing their luck.

It was on to the NLCS and a showdown with the Dodgers. Following the formula from the previous round, the Phillies took the first two at home but then dropped Game 3 on the road. On the night of Game 4, I was working at ArenaVision because the Flyers' season had started up by that point. And while I would never turn down being paid to watch the Flyers, my thoughts were wrapped up in that night's Phillies contest, which started some time during the second period of the hockey game. The Flyers and I lumbered through a 5-3 loss to Montreal, at which point I leapt into my car and sped home. The Phillies were losing by that same 5-3 score at that juncture of their game, and I made it home in time to see the top of the eighth inning.

More October magic was in the offing, as Victorino homered to tie the game. A few batters later, Matt Stairs came up as a pinch hitter to face another mass of humanity, Dodgers' reliever Jonathan Broxton. I probably don't need to remind you what happened, but I will. Stairs got a hold of one, big time. The camera couldn't tilt up high enough to catch the ball's trajectory, and I maintain that it is still in orbit over Dodger Stadium, possibly descending back to Earth around 2039. It was 7-5 Phillies, and the score would hold up, courtesy once again of Brad Lidge. The Phillies had one more win to go; the World Series was beckoning. Two nights later, another sterling start by Cole Hamels propelled the Phils to a 5-1 win to capture the pennant. Oh yeah.

Through a huge stroke of luck, the Phillies managed to avoid the Red Sox, who had lost to the Tampa Bay Rays in seven games in the ALCS. The Rays, in their first season after having shed the "Devil Rays" moniker, were an up and coming team, but still. The Rays! It was not lost on me that Tampa had won a Super Bowl and a Stanley Cup earlier in the decade, defeating Philadelphia teams both times along the way. As confident as I was in how the Phillies were playing, I was still prepared for the final insult: a Tampa Bay hat trick that would pretty much make me give up sports forever. And so it began.

The Series would start in Tampa thanks to MLB's wonderful "The All-Star Game winner gets home field" rule, and the teams earned a split. Back to Philly for three games. In my heart of hearts, I was feeling kind of gypped that the Phils would need to take all three in order to clinch the World Series at home, a challenging proposition, but I was really getting ahead of myself. I'd take whatever I could get at this point.

Because of rain, Game 3 didn't start until after 10pm, completely crippling the enthusiasm around it. I just wanted to go to bed but I wasn't going to miss a second of it. The Phillies blew a 4-1 lead but loaded the bases with nobody out in the bottom of the ninth, setting the stage for the crappiest walk-off hit in World Series history as Carlos Ruiz's 40-foot dribbler down the third base line was good enough to plate Eric Bruntlett for the win. It didn't hurt either that Rays' third baseman Evan Longoria basically threw the ball out of the stadium in a hurried attempt to get the force out at the plate. And with that, the Phillies had all the momentum heading into a pivotal Game 4.

Every so often, you get a classic pitching matchup in the postseason, like Sandy Koufax vs. Bob Gibson or Steve Carlton vs. Nolan Ryan. But this time we got Joe Blanton vs. Andy Sonnanstine. The Phillies took advantage of the so-so competition, jumping to a 5-1 lead after four innings. Pinch hitting for Sonnanstine in the top of the fifth, Eric Hinske (who was in the second of three straight years appearing in the World Series for three different teams) popped a home run to tighten the score to 5-2. But in the bottom of that inning, Joe Blanton secured his place in Phillies' lore.

After Pedro Feliz and Carlos Ruiz (The Killer Z's, as only I called them) were both quickly retired, Blanton came to the plate. Earlier in that 2008 season, a friend and I had traveled to Chicago to see the Phillies play a pair of games at Wrigley Field. At the park early enough to catch batting practice, I vividly remember watching Blanton take some hacks and giving the ball a ride to the warning track on a couple of occasions. This surprised me a bit because prior to coming over to the Phillies during that season, Blanton had spent his entire four-year career with Oakland, amassing only thirteen plate appearances before being traded from the AL to the NL. I remarked aloud that he looked like he could knock one out of the park if he got a hold of one.

And so, I can proudly say that to the surprise of every Phillies fan except for me, Blanton did indeed "get a hold" of a 93-mph Edwin Jackson offering, tomahawking it into the left field seats. It was the first home run by a pitcher in the World Series in 34 years and Blanton's ONLY EXTRA BASE HIT OF HIS ENTIRE MLB CAREER. A complete accident to be sure, but that's some good timing right there. Ryan Howard also mashed in this game, hitting two home runs and driving in five runs en route to a 10-2 Phillies romp. They now had a 3-1 series lead. There was no turning back now; it was either going to be a championship or a stunning collapse.

Monday, October 27, 2008. It should have been THE DAY. But Mother Nature had other ideas. With horrible weather looming, the Phillies got a pair of runs in the bottom of the first, and then the pesky Rays scored single runs in the fourth and sixth innings in the now driving rain to knot it up. And so began the great delay. The tarp wouldn't even come off the field the next day, so the resumption of the game got shoved to Wednesday the 29th. All of the down time allowed for rampant speculation about who would be coming in to pitch for Tampa and who the Phillies would counter with at the plate with Cole Hamels' spot in the order due up.

I had presumed all along that Rays' manager Joe Maddon would go with rookie phenom David Price. So far, Price had only appeared once in the series, in Game 2 way back on the 23rd, and so there was no reason on God's green earth that Maddon shouldn't ride Price in this one until his arm fell off. I was legitimately dreading this situation because I thought there was a decent chance that Price could go four innings, steal a win for Tampa and then be available down the road for a similar role in a potential Game 7. But much to my amazement and happiness, Maddon proved himself to be way dumber than I gave him credit for and sent Grant Balfour to the mound. Charlie Manuel, much maligned for his managerial skills, sent his best pinch-hitting option, Geoff Jenkins, up to the dish.

On a full count, Jenkins crushed a ball off the center field wall for a leadoff double, narrowly missing a home run. Two batters later, Jayson Werth provided a go-ahead hit. The Phillies had things set up just the way they needed in regards to the bullpen, but the lead was short-lived as Rocco Baldelli took Ryan Madson deep in the top of the seventh to tie the game 3-3. Madson then got into more trouble and had to be relieved by JC Romero. It was at this point that Chase Utley made one of the most iconic plays of his career as he fielded a bouncer up the middle, faked a throw to first and then threw home to nail clueless Rays' baserunner Jason Bartlett at the plate in a futile attempt to score. I shudder to think what might have happened if Tampa had gotten the lead at that point. Thanks to Utley, it was still tied.

In the bottom of the inning, Maddon STILL didn't put Price in and Pat Burrell led off the inning with a double off the wall. Déjà vu. It would turn out to be the final hit and the final at-bat of his Phillies career. Pinch-running for Burrell, Eric Bruntlett (who seemed to be in the middle of everything somehow for a few seasons) was plated two hitters later by Pedro Feliz. The Phillies had a 4-3 lead, and Romero held it after a clean top of the eighth. In the bottom half of the inning, Maddon FINALLY went to Price, who walked Utley but got two strikeouts to keep the Phillies from expanding the lead. Maybe you should have gone to the guy a little earlier, eh Joe? Horrible managing aside, it was Brad Lidge time.

With a man on second and two outs, ol' Eric Hinske came to the plate. This was it. Lidge, who had finished the regular season a perfect 41-for-41 in save chances, was 6-for-6 in the playoffs up to this point. He was simply automatic all season long, though there were close calls along the way. And if ever there was a time he'd blow one, I'd convinced myself, this was it. It just didn't seem real. As I frantically updated my AIM away messages (remember those?) to reflect my growing excitement, the count went quickly to 0-2. I'm glad Facebook wasn't as prevalent then; my phone probably would have melted.

And then it happened. Lidge got Hinske to flail at an off-speed pitch to end the game and send the whole Delaware Valley into a frenzy, the moment I had spent my whole life waiting for. Watching the game at home, I jumped into my dad's arms in an ill-advised move that nearly resulted in injuries to both of us. But it didn't matter. My girlfriend Rachael was even happy for me despite not being a Phillies fan herself…more on that later. I had no idea how to handle the avalanche of emotion. This moment felt like the validation of my entire existence. And none of it was thanks to Fox announcer Joe Buck, who delivered the final call with far less emotion than he had given to Randy Moss pretending to pull his pants down celebrating a touchdown during an NFL playoff game a few years earlier.

Of course, the real takeaway that will reside in the hearts of all Philadelphia fans forever was the call by the great Harry Kalas, which most people didn't hear in real time and were only treated to later. Just to remind you…

Brad Lidge stretches, the 0-2 pitch…swing and a miss! Struck him out! The Philadelphia Phillies are 2008 World Champions of baseballllllllllllll!

I got chills the first time, the second time, the 100th time, and when I typed this; and I will every time I hear it for the rest of my life. To make it extra special, they had set a camera up in the broadcast booth to capture the moment. I'd like to shake the hand of whoever had that idea. It was even enjoyable to see Philadelphia's least favorite son, Chris Wheeler, pumping his fists and dancing around alongside Harry. Mercifully he did so without saying a word, as someone important had clearly instructed him ahead of time to shut the hell up and not ruin Harry's call.

Well, that was the best. And I had the good fortune to be off for the next two days, meaning that I could spend October 30 going to stores and buying up all manner of championship merchandise, and then go to the parade on Halloween. I have always been a Halloween guy, collecting fake severed heads and the like since I was about eight years old. Yeah, I was a weird kid. Plus, what's not to like about the candy, the costumes and everything else? But on this particular October 31, All Hallows Eve was taking a big time backseat to the World Champion Philadelphia Phillies.

Thanks to my girlfriend, my dad and I were able to score a pair of tickets inside Citizens Bank Park for the culmination of the parade. I had actually managed to break through on the computer the previous morning and got tickets inside Lincoln Financial Field, but I gave them away to a friend after the ballpark tickets came up. And so we arrived at the Nova Care parking lot at about 7:30am on parade day and commenced an early morning tailgate of sorts. It was absolutely bizarre that we didn't have a game to look forward to. We had already won! What a feeling. A small part of me wanted to go out on the actual parade route, but the throng of humanity seemed imposing. I figured I'd save that experience for the next time.

We had cruised up 95 from Delaware in the normal amount of time, scoffing at the mayor's warning to take public transportation and not jam up the roads. How'd that work out anyway? Trains in Delaware were filling so fast that people in the Wilmington area were having to drive SOUTH just to board trains while there were still available seats. Maybe those unfortunate souls that got caught up in that whole situation viewed it as some kind of badge of honor, but I preferred our easy ride up and relaxing time in the parking lot as we grilled up some breakfast hot dogs and waited for the ballpark to open. During this time, I got a phone call from my employer and was asked if I was available to work that day. They had a callout and were looking for someone to come in. I nearly laughed them off the phone. I later found out that a big Phillies fan whom I work with had been the one who called out that day. Hmmm.

So, after our victory tailgate, we made our way over to the stadium to take in the festivities on PhanaVision. Perhaps some would claim that this didn't actually constitute going to the parade, but it was a picture perfect Halloween afternoon spent in the ballpark and I had my own seat instead of rubbing elbows with millions of Philly's sweatiest, so it was fine by me. I've never seen everyone so happy. The joy of the situation also made time seem to stand still, as I couldn't tell you if we were there for three hours or five hours or however long it was.

Eventually the parade found its way to Lincoln Financial Field, and then finally Citizens Bank Park. The entire organization was feted as conquering heroes as far as I can remember, except for pitcher Adam Eaton. He was booed like the crook and bum that he was. Harry the K fittingly emceed the whole thing, and it was awesome. Charlie Manuel endeared himself to

Philly fans forever with his disjointed yet touching words. Say what you will about Uncle Charlie, but he got the job done. I didn't think it was going to happen, but he proved all of us wrong. And he'll never be forgotten for what he did. And then came Chase Utley.

I don't know if Utley's wardrobe that day was inspired by Jesse Pinkman from *Breaking Bad* or the other way around, but he exuded his normal coolness as he came to the mic. Now, Chase MAY have had a beverage or two by this point, because he certainly seemed a lot looser than the workmanlike, nose-to-the-grindstone player we had come to love over the past few years. In a move straight from the 1980 parade where Tug McGraw exclaimed "New York City can take this World Championship and stick it, cuz we're #1!", Chase went one step further.

"World F'ing Champions!"

With those three simple words, Chase elicited the loudest ovation that will ever occur in a Philadelphia sports stadium, and with good reason. The man can teach a master class on the proper time and place to use the F word. I don't know if you've noticed, but PG-13 movies are now allowed to get away with one, and they always try to put it where it will have the biggest impact in the film. They can't just throw them around like an R-rated movie. I am convinced that they send the scripts to Utley and ask him where to put it. It was amazing. If I had a little kid with me, I wouldn't even have been mad. The local stations, airing it live and uncensored, should have all won regional Emmys on the spot. Simply put, it was the best F ever.

Following the raucous celebration, literally everybody in the Philadelphia area spilled out onto the streets. It was the largest mass of humanity that I had ever been a part of. And even though it took way longer than usual to get back to our car and 95 was a parking lot, more than doubling the usual 45-minute drive, none of that mattered. We all had a champion. I had all my Phillies swag to prove it. And I had a stockpile of memories that would last a lifetime.

Man, did that feel good. A mixture of joy, relief, accomplishment and all the other warm and fuzzy feelings that can fill your heart. I always said that if one of these teams could finally bag a title, I would be satisfied for a long time, and so I was going to do my best to avoid the greedy nature of humanity. But I was definitely hungry for more immediately. Everybody was. Luckily for all of us (for once), the sports calendar never stops and there was plenty more excitement to come in the near future.

7.

THE "GOLDEN AGE"

What a glorious feeling. The Phillies were on top, and so were all of us by extension. And not only did 2008 feature the first championship in my fan career, but it was tremendous for me on a personal level as I gained full-time employment and then started dating Rachael, who would ultimately become my wife. So yeah, that was good. For the first time that I could remember, my sports-viewing experience didn't feel like a dire "life or death" situation and I just sat back and enjoyed whatever happened.

Just as the Phillies were parading, the Eagles were midway through what seemed like an unremarkable season. A November tie against the Bengals, famous for Donovan McNabb's complete unawareness that ties could happen in the NFL, stuck them with a 5-4-1 record. Not bad, but still last place in the ultra-competitive NFC East.

The Eagles would go 3-2 over the next five games and entered the season's final week with an 8-6-1 mark. They faced a must-win against the hated Cowboys, but they also needed a ton of help in order to have a chance at the playoffs. Amazingly, that help arrived and everyone who needed to lose in the early games did, setting the stage for a win-and-you're-in against Dallas. Played on December 28, Christmas came three days late to Philadelphia that year as the Eagles obliterated the pathetic Cowboys 44-6, sliding into the postseason and befuddling Philly fans everywhere who couldn't believe the run of success that we were now having.

At this point, the Birds were playing with house money, and they made the most of it by scoring a win at Minnesota and then another at the Giants in a truly satisfying playoff victory. Then they seemed to completely run out of steam during the first half of the NFC Championship Game, as they were trailing the Cardinals 24-6. In my mind, the goal at that point was to just keep it respectable and at least go out swinging. But the team showed impressive fight and amazingly took a 25-24 lead early in the fourth quarter on a 62-yard touchdown catch by super rookie DeSean Jackson.

For a brief moment, there was a "team of destiny" feeling that crept in, but it was ultimately not meant to be, with Arizona orchestrating a soul-killing eight-minute drive that resulted in a touchdown and 2-point conversion which put them up 32-25, the eventual final score. The Cards would go on to lose the Super Bowl to Rachael's favorite team, the Steelers. And I was happy for her just as she had been for me a few months earlier when the Phillies had tasted victory. I also wanted the Cardinals to lose because I couldn't take another team winning a Super Bowl before the Eagles after being a laughingstock for much of their existence (see: Buccaneers).

Despite this missed opportunity, the city was still basking in enough of the championship glow to give the Eagles a pass. After all, they had impressively rallied to make the playoffs, including the sweet beatdown of the Cowboys in the season's final week, and then won two road playoff games, taking down the Giants in the process. If they weren't going to win it all, this was pretty much as satisfying as it could get. And so it's kind of sad to look back in retrospect and realize that this was the end for Donovan McNabb and pals, and these were the final playoff wins in Andy Reid's tenure as Eagles coach. We didn't know it at the time, but it was going to be a while before we got back to that level.

I continued plugging away at my freelance gig for ArenaVision, pulling cables around the building for sporadic Flyers and Sixers games, my work there becoming less and less frequent since I had full-time responsibilities elsewhere and really didn't feel like working six or seven days a week too often. On occasion, I would work my typical overnight shift for my regular job, come home and sleep from about 10 am to 3 pm, then get up and go to the sports complex for a game, following that up with another overnight shift. Now, as a broken-down man in his 30's, my joints ache just thinking about the effort I had to put in and how much I had to push myself. Work hard and establish yourself while you have youth on your side, that's all I can say. Because it gets real difficult, real fast.

As for that Sixers season, I think the Wikipedia recap of the 2008-09 76ers says it best: *The only two things memorable about the season is that the team went back to the classic uniform style the team wore in the 1980s, and the Sixers defeated the Chicago Bulls in a game played at The Spectrum, the teams home from 1967–1996.* They finished right at .500 and lost in the first round of the playoffs, the most average season ever. The less said, the better, but that season did feature the only known instance where I recall rooting directly against a Philadelphia team when I was at the game.

My old college buddy Matt and I were both working a Sixers-Mavericks game on Presidents' Day afternoon. We had plans to hang out at his place later, so we just wanted the game to be over with as soon as possible so we could traverse the icy roads and start an evening that would mostly feature beer and *The Simpsons*. As I mentioned before, it was already exasperating to work Sixers games to begin with, something that became doubly so if the game took a long time or (perish the thought) went to overtime. You can guess where this is going.

The Sixers, on a 7-game winning streak, had come roaring back with twelve straight points in the last few minutes of the game to tie it at 93-93 with eight seconds remaining. This was horrible. We didn't exactly want the Sixers to lose, but the most important thing was that the game end right then and there. Since the game was a close one, there had been a lot of timeouts and fouls in the late moments of regulation, and now the looming specter of overtime was threatening to extend our time at work by probably twenty minutes when you factor in stoppages and of course the potential of even more overtimes beyond the first one.

And so, as Dallas took the ball up the floor, it happened to me. I was actually rooting for a Philadelphia team to lose this game. The Sixers committed a foul and the Mavericks used a timeout, necessitating another pointless trip onto the floor to shoot the Sixers' dancers or whatever they had us doing at that juncture. After play finally resumed, the ball came to Dirk Nowitzki. This was it. The Mavs' big man drained a shot at the buzzer for the win, sending me and Matt home happy and the 14,000 paying customers home disappointed. It was great, and I'm not going to apologize for being happy the Sixers lost. They did it to themselves. Thank you, Dirk. But yeah, a forgettable season overall.

The Flyers, trying to build on their surprising playoff run the previous spring, had a solid regular season but screwed things up on its last day as they lost a home game to the Rangers, costing them home-ice advantage for their first-round series with the Penguins. And for the second straight year, the Flyers were frustratingly beaten by their cross-state rivals, this time in six games. It was all punctuated by the Flyers blowing a 3-0 lead in Game 6, which I missed because I was at a baseball game in Baltimore. Call me a bad fan I guess. Kind of glad I didn't have to deal with it though.

At least I will have the everlasting memory from December of that season when I took Rachael to her first Flyers game. I wasn't sure where our relationship was headed at that point, and I was hoping that I could coax her into being a serious Flyers fan. Her college roommate was big on the Flyers, so Rachael had at least a passing interest in them through this exposure, but I was really trying to make it stick. But through two periods of her first game, the Flyers were going through the motions and trailed the Carolina Hurricanes 5-1. I was fuming and found myself apologizing to her for how crappy the experience had been.

But when the third period started, the Flyers came out like a house on fire, with Scott Hartnell potting two goals to polish off a hat trick. They still trailed 5-3, but they scored twice in the last five minutes of the game to incredibly force overtime. Even more amazingly, they actually won in the shootout, which never happened. It was the greatest comeback that I had ever seen the Flyers make in person and one of the biggest in franchise history. All in Rachael's first game. I think this sealed the deal and minted her as a fan for life. Who knows, maybe we never get married if the Flyers sleepwalk through the third period. Sounds crazy, but they are such a big part of my life that I probably wouldn't get along too well with someone that had zero interest in them.

And so I'll cling to that first game I went to with Rachael, because that particular NHL season ultimately ended on a sour note. Six weeks after beating the Flyers in the playoffs, Crosby and the Penguins were hoisting the Stanley Cup and they were cemented in my mind as my least favorite sports franchise. The team that had been so poorly-run and out of money because nobody cared about them and who should have been playing in Kansas City or Seattle by then was laughing at us as they paraded down whatever cobblestone street runs through the middle of Pittsburgh while their tens of fans cheered them on, all because they were bad enough for long enough to get high picks in the draft and subsequently lucky enough that said picks came in years with slam-dunk superstars that any team could have had a run of success with. The 76ers seemed to take this same approach a decade later, and we'll see if trusting the process works out for them.

Of course, by the time that the winter teams were busy losing first-round playoff matchups, the Phillies had started their 2009 campaign and had officially begun their championship defense. Some months earlier as the offseason floated on, I found myself in the rarified air of full-blown taunt mode. After two straight years of Mets collapses opening the door for Phillies' division titles, I really wanted to rub salt in the wound of the team's biggest rival and wrote the following piece…

Mets Prepare to Choke Again in 2009 (1/13/09)

As the offseason winds down, there are only 32 days until Mets pitchers and catchers report to Port St. Lucie, FL , and begin choking.

In 2007, the Mets overcame their seemingly insurmountable seven-game division lead with seventeen to play and made choking history. Last season, they were able to put a strong July and August behind them to go 8-12 over the final three weeks, repeating their 2007 choke and passing Philadelphia in the loss column once again.

Now, with manager Jerry Manuel in place for his first full season at the helm, he believes that the team has made the necessary adjustments to continue choking in an increasingly competitive National League.

"To bring in a closer the caliber of Francisco Rodriguez, he will blend in nicely with our club dynamic. Throw in the alarming drop in his velocity and I have every confidence that he can perform the same way for us that Billy Wagner has over the past couple seasons."

Presumptive setup man J.J. Putz brings another interesting component to the Mets' bullpen. "Last year, it was rough, losing 100 games like that," said the former Mariner when reached for comment about his expectations for his new club in 2009.

"Our season was over by the All-Star break and it made it difficult to focus on your job every day when you feel like you have no chance. But here I know we'll have a shot, right down to the wire, probably even ending on the season's final day again."

At the same time, there is no question the Mets will miss the likes of Aaron Heilman, Scott Schoeneweis, and Joe Smith from their bullpen. "Those guys were key in what our bullpen accomplished in recent seasons," said Manuel.

"Still, it gives some younger guys a chance to choke and show the organization what they can do".

But while the Mets' pitching staff has seen a good deal of turnover, the offense figures to return largely intact with an experienced base of chokers that includes David Wright, Carlos Delgado, Carlos Beltran, and of course, Jose Reyes.

General manager Omar Minaya couldn't be happier with his shortstop. "Jose is just a special player, a real x-factor for our club".

"It's not just his natural ability. It's that clubhouse persona. It's the way he infuriates other teams with the things he does. I think he's the number one reason for our choking success of late".

So as the Mets begin a new chapter in their history this season with the opening of Citi Field, they again set out to prove their supporters wrong, and choke yet again when it matters most.

And, with Reyes and company still in place, they look capable of doing it for years to come.

I knew that this article had achieved its desired purpose when I got several angry comments from Mets fans and even had one make a fake profile using my name and likeness on the social site for which I had written the article, going on to post things in an attempt to get me in trouble. Needless to say, I had to contact site administrators. Mets fans, nothing but class.

As the 2009 season began, the Phillies got to be the center of the sports world, hosting the opening game against the Braves and wearing their fancy gold-pinstriped uniforms. Naturally, they lost. A few days later they held their championship ring ceremony, and once again Adam Eaton was fittingly booed. It was a beautiful time to be a fan of the team, when mere days later, tragedy would strike. Our beloved Harry Kalas passed away. With the Phils visiting DC for the Nationals' home opener, Harry was at the ballpark getting ready to do his job, like he had done so beautifully so many times before. And then, all of a sudden, he was gone. A great career and a great life, ended at age 73. Not a short life by any means, but one that definitely felt like it still had some mileage to run.

Despite the fleeting nature of our existence as human beings, there are some things that we just inherently hold to be true. For me, one of those things was that Harry would always be there calling Phillies games. It had been the case for over a decade before I had been born, and it remained so throughout my entire childhood and formative years, past college and beyond. And now it was over. His passing was one of the saddest days of my life. I cried. I met the man just once, but his death impacted me more than all but that of my closest family members. Writing about it the following day, I tried to put my feelings into a form that made sense…

What Harry Kalas Meant to Phillies Fans (4/14/09)

It is a sad time in Philadelphia. As David Montgomery said, "We lost our voice." But it's only during times like these that we realize how truly lucky we have been over the past 39 years.

Watching the Phillies will never be the same. And I don't think I'm being overly dramatic when I say my life in general will never be the same.

I am 24 years old. To me, Harry has always been there. He is the Phillies. And there are many other young Phillies fans who feel the same way. We have known nothing but Harry. We were spoiled.

In much the same way that we live vicariously through sports to begin with, broadcasters like Harry Kalas become our friends. We can depend on them game after game to be there for us, even when things are going wrong in our own lives.

It's a one-way dialogue, but when you are as good as Harry was, you truly make the listeners feel like they are experiencing the game with you.

Especially when he was paired with Richie Ashburn, Harry had a way of making it seem like you were sitting down with a couple of buddies enjoying a Phils game. Maybe you never met the man in your life, but if you were a Phillies fan, he felt like a great friend.

I have one personal story about Harry. In the summer of 2001, I went with some friends to Dorney Park in Allentown, PA, on the day before the MLB All-Star Game. Much to our amazement, we spotted Harry Kalas sitting on a bench, waiting for his grandchildren to finish a roller coaster ride.

We swarmed Harry and told him we were huge fans of him and the Phillies. Harry was probably taken aback that these 16-year-old kids were such fans of him. I wonder if it ever dawned on him how much he meant to so many young people because he had been a constant in their lives.

I also told him that his Hall of Fame induction was long overdue. But instead of stating his case and showing any kind of disappointment or resentment about having been left out for far too long, he was humble about it.

He said that he never expected to be in the Hall of Fame but instead would see it as a great honor to be enshrined after he saw how long it took his partner Whitey to achieve that milestone. He clearly had no sense of entitlement about it and was grateful just to be mentioned as a candidate.

I told Harry that I thought he would be inducted the following year and that I would go to Cooperstown to see it. He was, I did...and so did an army of thousands upon thousands of Phillies fans.

We as fans have a special place in our hearts for broadcasters because they are a direct link between us and the organization we so fervently support. Harry was a fan himself and wanted the Phillies to win just as badly as we did. We lived and died along with him.

If you thought it was difficult to get through those 2008 World Series Championship DVDs without breaking down before, just wait until you watch them again and see Harry celebrating among the millions of fans he brought so much joy to for decades.

We were just as happy to see Harry in that parade as we were for any of the players, because players tend to come and go, but we can spend decades enjoying someone like Harry.

He ended his Cooperstown speech with a poem, the last line of which was, "Philadelphia fans, I love you." Not as much as we loved you back, Harry. It will be difficult without you.

Outta here. But never to be forgotten.

Even today, as each new season dawns I still expect to see Harry in the booth and to hear him call the highs and lows of Phillies baseball. When I get really excited, I break out my slightly above-average impression of him. For me and my friends, he will live forever. How truly lucky we were to have him. Even someone who didn't have the good fortune to meet him in person would agree. His statue at Citizens Bank Park is my personal favorite because it honors a man who was there for me and breathed life into a whole generation of Phillies fans even when the team itself wasn't very good.

Some years later, I visited Harry's grave at Laurel Hill Cemetery in Philadelphia. I highly recommend it, even if you're not usually a graveyard-traipsing ghoul like I am. A giant microphone-shaped monument, flanked a few feet away on each side by blue Veterans Stadium seats, is a fitting tribute to Harry. It's also a reminder of the power that sports can have in our lives via the deep emotional attachments we can form to the people that enrich our experience as fans.

The Phillies seemed to be on a mission as 2009 carried on, if not directly motivated by Harry then at least buoyed by the idea of winning one for him. With 2008 in the rear view mirror, the city and Phillies fans everywhere rallied around this team in its bid to repeat. They didn't exactly run away with it, but they were on cruise control in July when the team signed Pedro Martinez as a free agent and then a few weeks later made a huge move by trading for ace lefty Cliff Lee.

In August, Rachael and I went to Chicago in what was her first trip ever to the city but my third straight year going to see the Phillies play at Wrigley. What a treat as usual. The Phillies won both games we attended, in wildly different ways. In the first one, Brad Lidge blew a save (yes, he turned into a human in 2009) but the Phillies gutted out a 12-inning win on a home run from Ben Francisco, who had just come over in the Lee deal. This game also represented perhaps the coldest I ever remember being at a sporting event. Again, this was August. But when you're dressed for summer in the last row at Wrigley in extra innings and the wind starts whipping around, it is not pleasant. I believe I told Rachael she'd be fine in shorts and to leave her jeans in the hotel. My bad.

The following day, Pedro took the mound for the Phillies. After hating him for years with the Mets, this was certainly bizarre to see in person. He pitched five decent innings, which was fine as the Phillies cruised to a 12-5 win on the strength of an 8-run 4th inning. The one image burned into my memory from this game was Shane Victorino making a catch in deep center and immediately being showered with a beer thrown by a Cubs fan in the bleachers. He almost missed the catch because of it, and I have no idea why the runner tagging from third was allowed to score without being sent back because of fan interference, but it didn't end up mattering. All you have to remember is that Cubs fans and all other fans are perfect angels, while Philadelphia fans continue to remain scum. This message brought to you by ESPN and the entire national media.

Less than two weeks later, I witnessed something truly amazing in person. I followed the Phillies to Citi Field to see them take on the Mets, my first ever trip to that park. After jutting out to an early 8-2 lead, the Phillies slowly lost their grip until the Mets had drawn to within two runs and had two men on base with nobody out in the top of the ninth. Nobody will believe me when I say that the thought of an unassisted triple play went through my mind, but it did. My dad had told me years before about a semi-pro game he was playing in when one had occurred in a very similar situation. It seemed like this would be as good a time as any, because the Phillies were within a hair's breadth of blowing this game and sending me home in a mood.

Sure enough, the Mets' runners took off on the 2-2 pitch, and future Phillie Jeff Francoeur acquiesced by hitting a line drive right at second baseman Eric Bruntlett. He made the catch, stepped on second, and tagged the runner who had started from first. Bam. Triple play. Game over. I knew it immediately but I'm sure the Met fans didn't comprehend what had happened or the hilarity of losing in such a way. If they had just stunk all day it would have been completely unmemorable, but for them to nearly stage a huge comeback only to see it dashed by just the second game-ending unassisted triple play in MLB history was well worth the trip up I-95 that day for the horde of Phillies fans in attendance.

Bruntlett's already colorful Phillies career became the stuff of legend, and I would later view the jersey he wore that day on display at the Baseball Hall of Fame in Cooperstown. It was only the 15th unassisted triple play to ever go down in the record books, making it even rarer than feats like a pitcher throwing a perfect game or a batter hitting four home runs. Who knows if I'll ever see one of these other exceptional accomplishments firsthand, but at least I'll always have this triple play thanks to Mr. Bruntlett. The way it happened could not have been any sweeter. It seemed to me that the Phillies were primed to win it all again.

Anyhow, the Phillies churned into the playoffs where they dispatched the Rockies in the first round. It was some gratifying redemption for 2007. They then beat the Dodgers in five games in the NLCS again. The highlight of that series came in Game 4, with the Phillies down a run entering the bottom of the ninth. In came Dodgers closer Jonathan Broxton, who was looking for some redemption of his own. After he recorded the first out of the inning, Matt Stairs came to the plate. Broxton walked him on four pitches, clearly crapping himself in fear after what had happened the year prior. He then hit Carlos Ruiz with a pitch but got Greg Dobbs to line out. With two on and two outs, Jimmy Rollins delivered perhaps the single biggest hit of his career, ripping a double to right field to chase home two runs, giving the Phillies the win and a 3-1 series lead. Man, the Phillies really owned Broxton. They'd cruise in Game 5 to book a return trip to the World Series and a date with the Yankees.

Few things in Philadelphia sports history have been as big of a tease as Game 1 of that Fall Classic. Cliff Lee completely mowed down the Yankees en route to a complete game and a 6-1 Phillies win. It seemed like a no-brainer, to quote my friend Mike during the Eagles' fateful final game at the Vet vs. Tampa, that "the rout was on". But what followed over the next three games was just ugly to watch. A horrible start by Cole Hamels and then a ninth inning implosion by Brad Lidge left the Phillies in a 3-1 hole in the series. Cliff Lee again baffled the Yankees for seven innings in Game 5 before running out of gas, but the Phillies held on for the win to keep hope alive.

But by this point, the "team of destiny" feeling that had been surrounding the Phillies for most of the year had faded and they would go down meekly in Game 6. What a gut punch to lose the World Series to the Yankees. Obviously it always hurts to get so close, but I legitimately felt that the 2009 Phillies were far better than the 2008 team and were perfectly equipped to repeat as champions. I guess that's why they play the games.

The Eagles looked to put some salve on fans' collective wounds in the aftermath of the Phillies' loss, ripping off six straight wins in November and December to carry an 11-4 record into Dallas for the season's final game with the NFC East title on the line. But the Birds wilted and lost 24-0, which then triggered a playoff rematch in Dallas the next week. They promptly lost 34-14, their third defeat at the hands of the Cowboys that season. It ended up being Donovan McNabb's last game as an Eagle, sending the team into a QB merry-go-round that would last more than half a decade. Perhaps the 2008 World Series had raised my expectations too high, because I was feeling all of these losses more acutely than I ever had before.

The Phillies managed to sneak in some crazy moves during their offseason, bringing in Cy Young winner Roy Halladay from Toronto. Under any other circumstances, such a trade would be cause for dancing in the streets. But the Phillies did the most Philadelphia thing ever and TRADED AWAY CLIFF LEE THE SAME DAY to Seattle for, as it would turn out, a big bag of crap. Were they loading up for another title or trying to replenish the farm system? Pick one, Amaro! Ahhhhhh!!!! Anyway, the net result was "I guess this is good" and then everyone kind of moved on and waited for the season to start.

Around this time, my excitement did start to boil over because Matt and I had scored tickets to see the Flyers play the Bruins at Fenway Park in the NHL's annual Winter Classic on New Year's Day. Well, I should say that I scored the tickets through my dad's friend. So on New Year's Eve morning we set out for Boston with the modest plan of staying just one night in the suburb of Dorchester, attending the game the next afternoon and then coming back to the Philly area late that evening.

The first phase went off without a hitch, with the only notable issue being that we literally couldn't find food where we were. All restaurants were serving a prix fixe menu and were booked. You know, because it was New Year's. Even McDonald's and the like had closed early that evening before we had crawled out of our hotel to go looking for grub and a place to have some drinks as midnight approached. Other than the empty calories from the alcohol we ended up consuming that evening, the lunch we had had at Cracker Barrel in the early afternoon would have to suffice until the morning.

I don't know how my stomach wasn't falling out but I was actually doing ok in the morning as we arrived at Fenway early to check out the festivities going on around it. Matt was a different story, as he had been voraciously hungry since the previous night. We finally managed to get some food at a stand outside the park. Matt bought two sausages and absolutely inhaled one of them before even getting to the register to pay. The game itself wasn't great, but the pomp surrounding it and the whole spectacle was amazing, perfectly accented by the Green Monster backdrop that I had a nice view of from my seat. For New Year's Day, it was so temperate that I didn't even put my gloves on until halfway through the game. Yes I was dressed for winter, but I still find it crazy that I was warmer at Fenway on January 1st than I had been at Wrigley in August.

One highlight in particular was the dueling "Let's go Flyers" and "Let's go Bruins" chants that the fans exchanged back and forth for a time. Philly fans always travel well, and it seemed to me that 30-40% of the crowd were Flyers supporters based on cheering volume and the tinge of orange that I saw in the stands. It was definitely a point of pride that this many people made the trip to fill seats that would have otherwise been occupied by Beantowners who had stumbled out of some Southie bar at 4am that morning. The lone moment of crowd unity came when someone started up a "Yankees suck" chant. It was fun for the whole family and really showed solidarity. The Yankees truly are the worst.

The Flyers clung to a 1-0 lead into the game's dying moments when of course the Bruins tied the game on a goal by former Flyer Mark Recchi. And then they won in overtime. The Flyers really weren't very good at that point and I should have expected it. It was a long subway ride back to our car and then an even longer car ride back to Philadelphia. Still, I was back in Delaware by midnight after having watched a hockey game in Boston that afternoon. The loss really didn't put too much of a damper on the whole experience, but man, it really would have been nice to come home a winner. More than anything, I was agitated by the Bruins' fans and their chirping on the way out of the game. And Boston fans in general. They were cordial enough all day but then felt the need to rub a regular season overtime win in our faces as everyone left. At that point in time, I was really hoping for a way to shut them up somehow.

As mentioned, the Flyers weren't exactly great that season, as they lived on the edge of the playoffs for much of it. Finally, everything came down to the last day of the regular season and a home date with the Rangers. The winner was in the playoffs and the loser would hit the golf course the next morning. This would be the biggest regular season game of my lifetime.

For two periods it was bleak, as Henrik Lundqvist stymied the Flyers at every turn and the Rangers clung to a 1-0 lead on an early goal by goon Jody Shelley. Incidentally, the Flyers were so impressed by this one goal that they signed Shelley in the offseason. But just when yet another loss seemed inevitable, Matt Carle scored in the third to tie the game. The teams stayed locked through regulation and then the overtime. Again, I waited for the other shoe to drop, as the Flyers had been nothing short of God awful in the five years since the NHL had adopted the shootout. Facing an all-world goaltender in this situation was just about the worst case scenario and part of me was wishing that the Flyers had just lost the game 5-2 and gotten it over with as quickly as possible rather than stretching my agony to the limit.

But incredibly, the Flyers were able to push two past Lundqvist, and Brian Boucher made the game-winning stop at the other end to catapult the Flyers into the playoffs. Even if just for a moment, it felt like a Stanley Cup win right then and there. To face down the biggest rival your franchise has ever had and ruin their season while simultaneously putting yourselves in the playoffs bordered on pure ecstasy. But I wasn't even worried about the playoffs; I just needed a cigarette.

That feeling of satisfaction gave way rather quickly to the "why the hell not?" mentality that accompanies rooting for a team with seemingly nothing to lose like the 2010 Flyers. In round one, they held the Devils to nine goals in five games, the series tilting on a Game 3 overtime winner by super pest Daniel Carcillo. Next up were those Bruins, and I was out for blood after the way the Winter Classic had ended. I really wanted to make those guys and their fans eat it. But it wasn't going to happen. At least not through the first three games, with the Flyers falling into the dreaded 3-0 hole. I had tickets to Game 4 and was just hoping to put one win on the board, much like during the 2008 East Final against Pittsburgh. I had never been on hand to watch my team's season end in person, and I didn't want to start now.

Spirits were about as high as they could be for fans of a team facing an insurmountable deficit, but the Flyers had given us a lot to be proud of that season and the crowd showed its appreciation. On this night, they would dart out to a 3-1 lead, only to cough it up in the third period. The Flyers scored to go back up 4-3 and the game reached its final minute when Mark Recchi (AGAIN) scored to tie it 4-4 with 32 seconds remaining. How demoralizing. I don't recall ever having a more deflated feeling at a Flyers game that was still up for grabs than I did at that moment and honestly didn't see how the Flyers were going to recover from it.

But Simon Gagne came to the rescue late in the first overtime, tipping home a point shot to extend the series and send me home a winner via OT in a playoff game for the first time in my life. It was a great thing to check off my bucket list, and it happened in the 23rd Flyers playoff game that I had ever attended. Yes, I went back and figured that out. But like most everyone else, I assumed that'd be it. The Flyers were still down 3-1 in the series and headed back to Boston.

But in that game, Michael Leighton picked up for an injured Brian Boucher and the two goaltenders combined for a 4-0 shutout. Back to Philadelphia. Those feelings were starting to stir. Again, why not? In Game 6, Leighton carried a shutout to the final minute. The Bruins got on the board, but the Flyers still won 2-1 to set up Game 7 back in Boston. Maybe it was time to adjust my expectations. Instead of preparing myself for the worst, perhaps I should start to believe that this team could overcome any adversity thrown at it.

This hypothesis was tested right off the bat, as the Flyers were overwhelmed by three Bruins goals in the first fifteen minutes of Game 7. At this point, Flyers coach Peter Laviolette took what stands as the greatest timeout in the history of sports. He rallied the troops and, as we later found out, impressed upon them that they couldn't make up the deficit all at once. They just needed to get one back before the end of the period. And they did, as James Van Riemsdyk scored two minutes later to stop the bleeding.

Goals by Scott Hartnell and Danny Briere in the first half of the second period tied the game and silenced the Boston crowd and the Bruins themselves. The teams played to a stalemate for more than a period after that, but you could tell it was just a matter of time. And for once, fate was on our side. After the Bruins took a too many men on the ice penalty, Simon Gagne scored the biggest goal of his life (surpassing the one from earlier in the week), snapping home a power play goal with 7:08 to go. It would hold up. The Flyers had posted a 4-3 victory in both Game 7 and the series as a whole after staring down 3-0 deficits in both of them. It was the most delicious piece of sports symmetry I have ever witnessed, and it took a spot right behind the 2008 World Series as the happiest sports experience of my life to that point. The 3-0 series comeback was just the third in NHL history, and it will be there for all-time for me and Flyers fans everywhere to look back on fondly. But hey, there was still more hockey to be played!

Somehow the Flyers managed to have home ice advantage for the Eastern Conference Finals because the Canadiens had been pulling off some magic of their own in the first two rounds. But despite facing another hot team, my confidence level in the Flyers was soaring sky high, and they rewarded it with a five-game victory. They blew Montreal's doors off 6-0 in the opener and then recorded another shutout in Game 2. After splitting a pair on the road, they came home for the clincher, and for the second time in my life I was on hand for Game 5 of the Eastern Conference Finals to watch the Flyers win the not-at-all coveted Prince of Wales Trophy and move on to play for the Stanley Cup. Check this out…May 25, 1997: Flyers 4, Rangers 2. May 24, 2010: Flyers 4, Canadiens 2. Things were aligned, but hopefully not too much because 1997 ended on the sourest of notes and I didn't want a repeat this time.

It was back to underdog status for the Flyers as they took on a very skilled but still inexperienced Chicago Blackhawks club for all the marbles. I waited with baited breath for Game 3 since we had tickets, hoping that the Flyers could at least get one win in Chicago before coming home. No such luck. Both team's offenses were clicking in Game 1 but the Flyers came up short in a heartbreaking 6-5 loss. That was their chance, and they missed it.

Strangely enough, they didn't even end up being the top story in town that night because Roy Halladay threw a perfect game against the Marlins that evening. Leave it to our teams to give us the mixed bag that they did here. I personally couldn't even celebrate Doc's amazing achievement much because the Flyers really let a golden opportunity slip through their fingers that night. Maybe Halladay could have saved such a sterling performance for later in the year, like October. At any rate, after the Flyers suffered a 2-1 loss in a much tamer Game 2, my dad and I were off to Game 3 and the air of trepidation that surrounded it.

The Flyers had already far exceeded everyone's wildest expectations, but that didn't mean the fans were going to sit on their hands in the first Stanley Cup Final game in Philadelphia since the debacle against Detroit thirteen years prior. The building was loud and the excitement was palpable. Danny Briere continued his amazing playoff run by opening the scoring in the first period. Then Chicago came back twice in the second to even the score 2-2 after two periods. Early in the third, Patrick Kane scored to put the Blackhawks ahead. The air whooshed right out of the building, much like it had on the Recchi goal a few weeks before. But the Flyers showed their resiliency yet again and took just twenty seconds to tie it 3-3 as Ville Leino popped one in. After sixteen-plus more minutes of white-knuckle hockey, the horn sounded at the end of the third and it was on to overtime.

The Flyers came tantalizingly close five minutes in, as a shot hit the post and then squittered (I'm counting it as a word) right along the goal line before Chicago netminder Antti Niemi covered it. Hearts were in throats everywhere. Unperturbed, the Flyers struck for the winner less than a minute later, with Claude Giroux redirecting Matt Carle's pass from the point. Niemi got a big enough piece of the puck to slow it down but it coolly slid across the goal line to send 20,297 Flyers fans into pandemonium, myself of course included. It was the happiest single sports moment that I had ever witnessed at a game in person. I had no voice the next day.

The Flyers also took Game 4 to ostensibly make the series a best-of-3, although I didn't see much of it because by this point I was working evenings so I was simply out of luck on those nights. I caught what I could while I was on break, but I was largely removed from the action. There had been a smattering of games throughout the season that I saw little to none of, but they all paled in comparison to having to sit this one out. It sucked, not being able to fully enjoy it. I was actually off the night of Game 5, but it ended up being a mistake to even watch the game in the first place. Chicago rode a three-goal first period to a 7-4 win to set up Game 6, which again I wasn't going to be able to see very much of because of work.

I'm sure to many people it seems childish that a 25-year old would be so upset to miss most of a game because they were fulfilling a professional obligation, even a highly important game like the one in question. But I was dying inside. If the Flyers had been up 3-2 with a chance to clinch, I would not have been at work that evening. No matter what I had to do, I'd be watching it at home, and work could just deal with it. But in this case, they were down 3-2 and merely trying to prolong the series. I did catch a bit of it, but in perhaps the cruelest turn of the knife that I've ever had to suffer as a Philadelphia sports fan, I was not watching when Patrick Kane scored his infamously terrible goal in overtime to win the Cup for Chicago and dash the Flyers' dreams. I had to hear it from someone else, and with all the confusion surrounding the goal itself, was in a state of disbelief until I saw the replay a short time later.

As far as the feelings that sports can induce in us, that was pretty much as bad as it gets. A tremendous playoff run shouldn't end in heartbreakingly ugly fashion like that, but sadly it often does. It took several years for me to be able to watch that replay again, and even now I tend to avoid it or look away when it pops up for whatever reason. For me, it's even worse than Joe Carter. I had now seen both a World Series loss and a Stanley Cup Final loss in a span of less than eight months. As fans, we get tested in different ways by our teams from time to time, and this was definitely the biggest one-two gut punch I had ever taken.

*

8.

WELL, THAT WAS QUICK

A few weeks into my Stanley Cup (or lack thereof) hangover, I received a letter in the mail with ArenaVision's familiar letterhead on it. Apparently they were evaluating their freelance pool and I was among those being cut from the list. To be fair, I hadn't been all that available for the past couple seasons, maybe giving them three or four dates a month as I tried to navigate my full-time job, a social life and Flyers games that I already had tickets for. Still, I thought I deserved better than the four-sentence (one sentence for each year I worked there!) form letter that they sent. I was disappointed but not shocked. They had been getting cheap anyway, as employees no longer got a free pre-game meal. I had had a couple vending machine dinners in the last year I worked there, and I wasn't keen on having many more.

Oh well, it was fun while it lasted. I got to share an elevator with people like Brian Propp, met Lauren Hart before she sang the national anthem and bumped into Mike Emrick in a bathroom. I ate dinner with longtime Flyers public address announcer Lou Nolan and even got to hang in the decrepit old PRISM control room in the bowels of the Spectrum while I worked a few Phantoms games. Met some people, got some stories, didn't make all that much money. It was worth it overall.

As 2010 moved along, I hoped that the Phillies would ease my pain once again, with Halladay and company setting their sights on a third straight World Series berth. In June, Bill and I attended an interleague game against the Blue Jays that had originally been scheduled to be played in Toronto, so the Phillies were the road team. It was weird. Shortly after, the two of us took a road trip to Cincinnati to see the Phillies play a pair of games against the Reds. The Phillies won the first game in extra innings despite the ghost of Brad Lidge blowing a three-run lead in the bottom of the ninth.

As Bill and I crossed the river into Covington, Kentucky to go drinking after the game we saw several already banged up Phils fans in the Taco Bell drive thru. On foot. It was a proud moment to witness before we painted the town. The next day's game was an afternoon contest and I wasn't feeling 100%, but at least I was functioning better than Bill, who slept for half an hour in the last row of the stadium in the shade to avoid the midday sun that was baking our seats a few dozen rows below. He woke up in time for first pitch and we moved down to watch an unmemorable Phillies loss. But at least it was quick, and we were speeding out of the Cincy area by 3:30 for a trip that didn't get us back into Delaware until after 1am. I tried to "ice" Bill with a loose Smirnoff Ice that was rolling around in the trunk for some reason, but he declined to imbibe and our road trip was over.

2010 also marked the first year that I could call myself a Phillies season ticket holder, as I went in on a 17-game plan with a guy at work (we'll call him Rich) and we divvied them up between us. As the playoffs approached, we faced the quandary of how to split them since partial plans were only entitled to one game per round. It was decided that since it was Rich's idea to begin with, he would get tickets to the first round and I would be able to go to NLCS if the Phillies got there. Actually, WHEN they got there. It was a foregone conclusion.

The Phillies drew the Reds in the opening round, so it really made the whole "Red October" thing that the team was pushing seem kind of stupid. Either way, they were going to mop the floor with Cincinnati, and Rich was going to Game 1 with our tickets. In an event that annoys me to this day, Halladay made good on my "come through when it counts" request and threw a no-hitter, just the second in baseball postseason history. My interest in going to the NLCS had made me completely write off the first round, and I definitely could have been at that game if I had pushed for it. So I really couldn't enjoy this Halladay pitching outing either. It was fun and all, but I was truly hoping the Reds would eek out some lousy hit to break it up as I watched from home. As predicted, the Phillies swept the Reds aside to set up an NCLS showdown with the Giants.

At this point, the three-headed monster of Halladay, Cole Hamels and in-season addition Roy Oswalt looked unstoppable. But the teams split the first two games in Philadelphia, the Giants took Game 3 at home and then the Phillies blew a 4-2 lead in Game 4 to fall into a 3-1 hole. They staved off elimination in Game 5 to come back home, and I was going to be there for Game 6. Ever since getting my NLCS tickets, I was stoked at the prospect of possibly watching the Phillies clinch that night. My only fear was that maybe they would be too good and the series would be over before then. But I was clearly getting ahead of myself, as it was now time to watch nervously and hope against hope that they could win just to set up a seventh and deciding game.

It looked really good early on, with the Phillies plating a pair in the bottom of the first. But inexplicably that was all they would muster for the game. The Giants got two of their own in the third, putting all the fans in the park on edge as we collectively waited for the crushing blow to come. It arrived in the eighth inning in the form of a solo home run by San Francisco's Juan Uribe, moving the Giants ahead 3-2. It stayed that way until the bottom of the ninth. With two on and two out, Ryan Howard looked at a called third strike to destroy all hopes and end things on an ignominious note. I couldn't imagine a worse way for a season to end for Howard and the Phillies. It was the first time I had ever been there in person when one of my team's seasons ended, and I really don't want to experience it again. But this team was still loaded and I was sure they'd be back the next year with a vengeance.

In the fall of 2010, Michael Vick took the city and the NFL by storm. As controversial a signing as there had ever been in this town because of his checkered past, Vick won people over with a near-MVP performance to lead the Eagles to the NFC East title with a 10-6 record. The highlight of that season occurred during a pivotal December contest at the Meadowlands with the Giants. I was watching the game with friends and was probably going to have to leave a little early because I had work that evening. When the Eagles fell behind 31-10 with a little over eight minutes to play, I peaced out. Tempted to not even turn it on as I drove into work, I didn't want to miss the opportunity to take some perverted pleasure in hearing Merrill Reese bash how the Eagles had played, so I flipped it on. The Eagles scored a touchdown on the second play of their next drive to make it 31-17. I started to press down on the gas a little harder with about fifteen miles to go until I got to work.

The Eagles then recovered the onside kick. After five plays, they had scored to make it 31-24. I was definitely breaking the speed limit at that point. The Eagles stopped the Giants and got the ball back with three minutes to play. Then, after an eight-play drive, Vick hit Jeremy Maclin for the score and the Eagles had tied it up. I was getting close to work and was desperately hoping to run in and catch the end of the game before my shift started. I heard the Giants go three-and-out just as I roared into the parking lot and hustled in to watch overtime. After all, they were punting with just 14 seconds left. What was going to happen? I arrived inside just as my co-workers' cheering had died down from celebrating DeSean Jackson's game-winning 65-yard punt return touchdown as time expired. It was an amazing moment, and I missed it. Later I'd hear Merrill's call and Mike Quick's "This is Miracle at the Meadowlands number two!" I still feel cheated having not seen or heard this live. It's almost like it didn't happen. Nevertheless, this Eagles team looked like it would be a tough out in the playoffs.

The Eagles would go on to draw a difficult matchup with the Packers in the first round. They didn't have it in them, and a sluggish start doomed the Eagles, who never recovered from a 14-0 first half deficit in a 21-16 loss. Playoff failure had once again tainted a successful campaign. The Packers went on to run the table, winning two more road games and then the Super Bowl. Their five-point margin over the Eagles was the smallest of any of their four playoff victories. And I have to say that after all these years, I'm still torn. If you have to lose, do you want it to be to the eventual champion so you can at least say that you were beaten by the best? Or do you just want that team to lose as punishment for beating you? I really think about these things too much.

The 2010-11 76ers would have a very "Sixery" season, finishing 41-41 and then managing one win in a first-round loss to a loaded Heat team. But surprisingly, Miami didn't win it all that year, losing in the Finals to Dallas. Meanwhile, the Flyers won their first division title since 2004, then needed seven games to squeeze past Buffalo in the opening round. The Bruins were up next and were out for blood after the Flyers' historic comeback had stunned them the previous spring. The Flyers got them right where they wanted them again, losing the first three games. But history would not repeat itself, as the Bruins stomped the Flyers 5-1 in Game 4 to sweep the series and exact their revenge.

Six weeks later, there was a Stanley Cup parade in Boston as the Bruins snapped an even longer Cup drought than the Flyers, totally wiping away the ghosts of their dual 3-0 collapses from 2010. So from that point forth if you ever tried to bring up how amazing the 2010 Flyers' achievement was in overcoming 3-0 deficits to Boston in the series and in Game 7, Bruins fans and everyone can remind you "Yes, then that same team destroyed you the next year and went on to win the Stanley Cup". We can never have nice things.

During the Phillies' offseason, Ruben Amaro Jr. realized the folly of his ways and re-signed Cliff Lee, giving the Phillies an absolutely stacked rotation of four aces. And Joe Blanton.

Poor Joe. Blanton would go down in May with an injury, but rookie Vance Worley picked up the slack and was great as the fifth starter. Oswalt was only adequate but the Halladay-Hamels-Lee troika were all outstanding. The offense was strengthened with the arrival of deadline acquisition Hunter Pence, and the team was all set. It was an absolute juggernaut, finishing with 102 wins despite a late-season 8-game losing streak as they were rotating the regulars in and out to get them some rest before the postseason. The Phillies did, however, make a critical mistake. They swept the Braves over the season's final weekend, allowing the always pesky Cardinals to sneak past Atlanta for the wild card spot, setting up a first round matchup with St. Louis. The Phillies had gone 3-6 against St. Louis during the regular season, the only NL team they were below .500 against in 2011. Off we went.

Things started off right with an 11-6 victory in Game 1, and then I was going to Game 2 as the Phillies looked to take a stranglehold on the best-of-5 series. The Phillies quickly built a 4-0 lead against Cardinals' ace Chris Carpenter, but something still felt off. True, it was a chilly October night, and that sometimes neutralizes fan involvement and can quiet a crowd. But this was the playoffs and our team, the best in baseball, was about to go up 2-0 in the series. Phillies fans had actually become complacent.

It hit me all at once that the franchise's unprecedented run of success over the past couple years had spoiled us, which was nearly unfathomable to a Philadelphia fan. The desire to win was still there, but the trademark passion of the town's fans was not. If ever there were an argument for how a team could feed off the home crowd's energy, this game was it. The fans just weren't there and, after the second inning, neither were the Phillies.

The reliable Cliff Lee was touched for three runs in the fourth inning and then another in the sixth as St. Louis tied the game while the fans sat in stunned silence. Lee came back out for the seventh, a big mistake by Charlie Manuel, and promptly surrendered a leadoff triple, an RBI single and then another single before being removed. The Phillies' offense managed one measly hit in six innings off the Cards' bullpen in a 5-4 loss that should have never come to pass. Yes, the series was merely tied, but it felt then and there that the Phillies had just blown their chance. I don't want to be the guy to lay the loss squarely at the feet of Lee, but he came up tiny when his best was needed. Scratch that, the 4-0 lead didn't even merit his best work, just six or seven decent innings would have been fine. He didn't get the job done.

But as I mentioned, the offense mailed it in that night and so did the fans. I walked out of the building that night angry at the team but sorely disappointed in the fans that were there. Since the Phillies had started tasting success, CBP had largely become a hangout for college kids and other young people to treat a game as a social event rather than actually caring about what was happening on the field. Throw in the October weather, and it added up to very few people actually being "into the game" for this particular playoff contest. Each and every person at Game 2 should be ashamed for the lack of excitement in the building that night. Yes, I will take a hit on this too but I was literally yelling at the crowd to get going early in the game. One man can only do so much.

The Phillies recovered to win Game 3 in St. Louis, but they lost Game 4 when Roy Oswalt got distracted by a squirrel. Really. That's a bit of an oversimplification, but either way it set up a Halladay-Carpenter pitching matchup for a deciding fifth game in Philadelphia. It was another one of those evenings where I was at work and could only catch snippets of the game. The Cardinals led 1-0 after the second batter of the game, and then the zeroes started to pile up. Every time I got to tune in for a minute or check the score, the Phillies' proverbial "end of the line" seemingly drew nigh. Carpenter carried a three-hit shutout into the ninth inning. Just like the year before, Howard came to the plate as the Phillies' last hope. That called third strike against the Giants was about to look like a walk in the park.

Howard topped a ground ball to the right side and stumbled out of the box, tearing his Achilles tendon in the process. He valiantly got up, but it was basically the most painful thing a Philadelphia sports fan ever had to watch as he was thrown out by plenty before crumpling back to the ground in agony as the Cardinals danced all around the field to celebrate their victory. It was devastating, and even the most heavy-handed hack Hollywood writer wouldn't have laid on the symbolism this thickly. There lay Howard, a mammoth of a man and one of the driving forces of this Phillies mini-dynasty, felled on the final play of a season that should have ended with a World Series victory for the heavily favored ball club. We learned the hard way over the next few seasons that this was the end of Howard's productive years and the last gasp for those Phillies teams. And of course it probably goes without saying, but St. Louis would go on to win the World Series in 2011.

Roy Halladay had pitched remarkably in defeat but was denied along with the rest of the team in their bid to reach a fourth straight NLCS. It was yet another incremental step backward since the 2008 World Series. When Halladay tragically passed away in a plane crash seven years later, his perfect game and playoff no-hitter were of course the most fondly recalled memories by Phillies fans paying tribute to him. However, his performance in Game 5 was right up there on the list of his best ever. It was easily good enough to get his team a victory, but it just didn't happen. It is truly a shame that Halladay never got to pitch in, let alone win, a World Series.

The magnitude of the loss, both in this game specifically and in the series as a whole, can never be overstated. It was a brutal blow, even by Philadelphia sports standards. I rank the final out and Howard's injury right up there with the Scott Stevens hit on Eric Lindros as the single worst sports moments of this century in this town. And even with the 2008 World Series title in tow, I look back on this time period and am bitter that the Phillies came away with just one championship. 2008 was a great ride, and luck was on their side for once. But were they the best team that year, the one that definitely SHOULD HAVE won it all? Not really. In both 2009 and 2011, they should have won. And I would gladly trade 2008 for both of those years any day.

The Phillies had thrilled a new generation of Philadelphia fans, but they truly had spoiled us too much. The cyclical nature of sports dictates "what goes up, must come down". It was about to ring true for the Phillies, but we needed to hold out hope that the rest of our teams would lift our spirits back up. Instead, we were all about to embark on a rough ride that would truly test our fortitude as fans and stretch our collective patience and sanity to its limits.

*

9.

WHY DO I EVEN BOTHER?

As the 2011 Phillies rolled along toward what would ultimately be a franchise-shattering playoff disappointment, the winds of change blew through the Flyers' organization. On one single day in June, the team detonated its core. They sent their two best overall players, Mike Richards and Jeff Carter, out of town in separate trades. This by extension freed up enough salary cap space for the Flyers to sign goalie Ilya Bryzgalov, whose rights they had acquired from the Coyotes a few weeks prior because he was scheduled to become a free agent at the end of the month and would not re-sign there. Underachieving on the ice and a divided locker room apparently led to the seismic movement. Ed Snider, Paul Holmgren and company were taking big gambles that the package of players they received back in the deals would infuse the team with new life and that Bryzgalov was finally THE GUY in net.

The team's hopes were dealt an early, crippling blow as captain Chris Pronger took a careless stick to the eye in a game on October 24. Accidental, yes. But a completely careless follow through of a shot, which doesn't even qualify for a penalty by NHL standards. It was a horrifying sight, but the ultra-tough Pronger returned two weeks later and all seemed fine. However, he still wasn't right and was taken out of the lineup again after playing in just five more games. He never returned. The 37-year old Pronger had logged a ton of miles in his Hall of Fame career but still had plenty left in the tank that would go unused, as he was forced into an early retirement because of the injury.

During Pronger's first stint out of the lineup when we all thought his absence would be just a temporary setback, I attended a game against the reborn Jets, who were back in Winnipeg after the NHL had relocated the hapless Atlanta Thrashers there before the 2011-12 season. I had never seen the Jets play in person in their previous incarnation (they moved to Phoenix in 1996), but I was able to check this version off my list early. I am a total completist, as you can probably discern if you've gotten this far in the book, and I make it a point to see every NHL and MLB team in live game action.

The Flyers scored first in the game, but Winnipeg followed with an onslaught against Flyers' goalie Sergei Bobrovsky and took a 5-1 lead early in the second period. Bryzgalov, who had played like a sieve in a sloppy 5-1 loss the previous night, was summoned from the bench as coach Peter Laviolette seemingly just wanted to keep the game from turning into a total embarrassment. But the Flyers responded and sprung to life, drawing to within 6-4 by the end of the second period. The third period then started with a flurry the likes of which I had never seen, as the Flyers pounded home three goals in the first 3:02 to take a 7-6 lead.

Still, Bryzgalov and the defense in front of him couldn't hold it. The lead lasted all of 28 seconds, then Winnipeg broke the 7-7 tie just 1:01 after that. The Flyers did tie it late, but the Jets potted the final goal with 1:06 to play, as they won 9-8. It was the most insane game I had ever been to. Entertaining for sure, but it raised huge red flags about the team's goaltending and the state of the defense without Pronger anchoring it. The team's two Russian "B" netminders had combined to make just 16 measly saves on 25 shots, and we got our first glimpse of Bryzgalov's psychological state after the game as he made bizarre comments and seemed totally worn out both physically and mentally.

Bryzgalov's idiosyncratic nature was easier to swallow when he was playing well, and he did get things back on track in the games that followed. The Flyers, looking like they were about to fall off a cliff after the Winnipeg loss, rebounded and even ripped off a 7-game winning streak in December as another appearance in the NHL's Winter Classic approached, this time at "home" versus the Rangers at Citizens Bank Park. Naturally, I wanted to go. Matt had a beat on some tickets that we had talked about back in the summer, and ever since August I had fully been expecting to be there on January 2 for the game. Yes, January 2, since the 1st was a Sunday and the NHL didn't want to get crushed by week 17 of NFL football on that day.

Speaking of which, the Eagles wrapped up a forgettable 8-8 season that New Year's Day, one that they won the final four games of when things didn't matter and it only hurt their draft position to do so. They ended up finishing just a game behind the 9-7 Giants for the NFC East title, but New York would go on to win their second Super Bowl over New England in five seasons. They weren't very good, but they got hot at the right time. Must be nice.

As the Winter Classic approached, the mid-level tickets I was hoping for went down the tubes and I didn't want to spend $400 to go, so I missed out. I had been sated by going to the

Classic two years earlier in Fenway, so I wouldn't say the disappointment was too great, but it still would have been fun to attend. In retrospect, however, it's probably a good thing that I didn't end up going because the Flyers blew a 2-0 lead to the Rangers en route to a 3-2 loss. I had a bunch of people over to watch the game and tried to at least show some restraint, but it really pissed me off. I merely had to take solace in the Flyers' win in the alumni game the day before, highlighted by a barely-moving Bernie Parent playing the first couple minutes of the game due to overwhelming fan appeals and then getting a godlike sendoff when he was replaced in net. It was awesome, and I should have just made it my mission to be there for that game. And it bears repeating, Bernie is the best.

For the second straight season, HBO covered the Winter Classic and the weeks leading up to it with their *24/7* series. Ilya Bryzgalov became the undisputed star of the show, making even further weird statements about the universe and random subject matter. Then he didn't even end up playing in the game. The Rangers, of course, were presented as saints on earth, playing hockey in between humanitarian trips to leper colonies and saving kittens from trees. The Flyers were just some dudes. So the Rangers' win seemed like what the league and HBO wanted all along. Happy new year.

A few months later, Rachael and I took a trip to Toronto and I was able to achieve one of my lifelong sports goals of seeing the Flyers take on the Maple Leafs for Hockey Night in Canada. Bryzgalov pitched a shutout as the Flyers won 1-0 in a shootout. Maybe this guy would be fine after all. When the seedings fell into place for the playoffs that year, the Flyers would again butt head with the Penguins in a matchup where nobody was giving them a chance to win even though they had taken four of six meetings during the regular season with their cross-state rivals.

The series started as badly as could possibly be imagined, with Sidney Crosby getting the first goal in the opening minutes and the Penguins building a 3-0 lead in the first period. Although the situation wasn't completely as critical, it had shades of Game 7 in Boston two years prior. But the Flyers settled down, held the Penguins' offense in check the rest of the game, and would send it to overtime at 3-3 thanks to a pair of goals by Danny Briere. First-year Flyer Jakub Voracek then struck in overtime to give the Flyers an unlikely Game 1 win.

Game 2 turned out to be even more ridiculous, with Crosby taking a mere 15 seconds to open the scoring. The teams traded goals at a frantic pace and things were tied at 4-4 entering the third. Pittsburgh scored first, but the Flyers took it from there, with Sean Couturier and Claude Giroux both polishing off hat tricks on the way to an exhilarating 8-5 win. Things shifted to Game 3 in Philadelphia. It was a game that I would have killed to be at. In a fight-filled affair that featured over 150 combined penalty minutes, including a Crosby-Giroux dustup, the Flyers prevailed 8-4 to take a 3-0 series stranglehold. But any thoughts of a sweep quickly went down the crapper in the next game, with Pittsburgh winning 10-3. These teams could simply not play defense.

In Pittsburgh for Game 5, they finally clamped down and the Penguins won 3-2 to send things back to Philadelphia for Game 6. It was getting too close for comfort at that point. Someone was going to need to step up. Giroux did just that. Throwing his hat into the ring as "league's best player", he bowled Crosby over on the first shift of the game and then scored just 32 seconds in to set the tone. The Flyers never looked back, winning 5-1 to vanquish their rivals and send them crying back to Pittsburgh. Early defensive shortcomings aside, it was an encouraging result, and the team looked set up nicely in the Eastern Conference after the dust settled elsewhere in the first round.

Round two brought the Devils and, frankly, a series that the Flyers should win. The Flyers won the opening game in overtime, but then proceeded to drop four straight, scoring just seven goals in the process. After shooting fish in a barrel against Marc-Andre Fleury in the first round, their offense just couldn't crack longtime nemesis Martin Brodeur. Just like that, the good vibes from the unbelievable first round victory over Pittsburgh were washed away and things were again unsettled in Flyers country, as they are every single spring. Those Devils would make a surprise run to the Stanley Cup Final before they were thankfully stopped by the Kings. Three Cups is more than enough for that team.

That year's Sixers were a decent squad, posting a 35-31 record in a NBA season that had been abbreviated by a labor dispute. They were good enough to sneak into playoffs as the East's #8 seed, but they faced the top-seeded Bulls, led by reigning MVP Derrick Rose. The Sixers predictably lost Game 1, but they got what they needed as Rose went down with an injury that would keep him out for the rest of the series. The door was open, and the Sixers took full advantage. They played suffocating defense for the rest of the series, allowing less than 81 points per game over the next five contests in a stunning six-game upset.

Andre Iguodala, playing in his eighth and final season as a Sixer, sealed the deal with two seconds left in the final game, knocking down a pair of free throws to turn a one-point deficit into a one-point lead that would prove to be the difference. I was genuinely into it as I watched, as this was all happening right around the same time the Flyers were going down in flames against the Devils (pun maybe intended) and I needed something to hold onto. The Cinderella story would halt in round two, however, as the Celtics beat them in a hard-fought seven game series where the teams alternated wins. It was a fairly heartening wrap to the season for an overachieving 76ers squad, but dark days were ahead for both them and the rest of the city's teams as a whole.

You wouldn't have known it at the time, but the Sixers were about to enter a period of unprecedented bad basketball that included five straight years without a whiff of the playoffs and a couple very serious runs at the NBA's single-season loss record. As for the overall state of Philadelphia sports, the 2011-12 Sixers' first round playoff victory would be the last time that any of the city's major pro teams advanced past the first round of the postseason until 2018. We'll get to that one a little later.

When Rich and I had divvied up our Phillies' tickets earlier in 2012, we didn't realize it was the beginning of the end. I didn't much care which games I ended up with and just tried to pick ones that worked around my schedule, and one such game was an August matchup with the Reds. It fell on what figured to be an off day for me and also featured a Hunter Pence bobblehead giveaway. I asked for that game, Rich said it was fine, and we agreed on all the games in our plan without issue, just like we had the previous two years. But a day or two later, I was surprised that he entreated me to let him have the Reds tickets because his wife wanted to go to that particular game. Longtime Phillies reliever Ryan Madson was apparently her favorite player and had signed with Cincinnati that offseason, so she really wanted to see him.

I pointed out the folly of going to a game to see a relief pitcher who probably had less than a 50/50 shot of actually pitching. But our tickets were in fact near the bullpen, so she could gaze lovingly at Madson even if he didn't enter the game. I reluctantly agreed to let him have those tickets but asked that he give me one of the Pence bobbleheads. And while I don't remember a convincing "yes" from him, he didn't refuse me either. As I forked over the tickets, I remarked that Madson would probably be hurt by then anyway, rendering the whole stupid situation pointless.

Lo and behold, the Phillies stunk up the joint that year and actually traded Hunter Pence at the deadline, some three weeks before the date of his bobblehead giveaway. And Madson blew out his elbow in spring training, never appeared in a regular season game for the Reds, and wouldn't even pitch in another MLB game until 2015. Yet I heard nothing from Rich about giving the Reds tickets back to me even though the reason he gave me for wanting that game was no longer valid. By the time the Cincinnati game finally rolled around, I didn't care about the tickets or the bobblehead. I don't even remember what the Phillies ended up doing about that promotion. You see, I had something a bit more important going on right then. I got engaged.

After four-plus years of dating, everything finally seemed right and I proposed to Rachael. The joyous occasion was a welcome oasis in the rapidly drying desert that was Philadelphia sports. Those 2012 Phillies had a Sixers-like .500 finish and missed the playoffs for the first time since 2006. And on a tragic note, Andy Reid, entering his fourteenth season as Eagles head coach and firmly on the hot seat, suffered the cruelest loss of all when his son passed away during training camp in August. Mere days later the Eagles played their first preseason game that year, and I was there as a freelancer to work at Lincoln Financial Field. Matt had used his connections and managed to get me in with the production company that ESPN had hired to produce Monday Night Football that season. I was excited to be a part of it, although I didn't know exactly what I'd be doing for the game or if I could parlay it into something more than a single appearance.

Before the game, I spent some time along the sidelines so I thought I'd be running cables, helping the camera operators or otherwise employed like I had been with ArenaVision. But at some point I got delegated to gopher duty and had to run stats and other printouts from the production truck to someone inside the building. It was a back and forth that involved the parking lot and the bowels of the stadium, and it was really disappointing that I didn't get to be in the truck, on the field or in the stands. The specifics escape me because it was such a lousy experience. I didn't expect to wow them so much that they gave me a full-time job or anything, but they clearly had more people than they knew what to do with and had to hand out busywork to some of them.

I do recall being made to watch over a luggage cart in the parking lot late in the game, and one of the bags had a tag that said "Joe Theismann" with a phone number listed right next to the name. I resisted the strong urge that I had to put the number in my phone and make random crank calls to a Super Bowl-winning quarterback turned broadcaster, and I guess that karma paid off as I bumped into Joe Theismann five years later at the Memphis airport of all places. I took a couple pictures with him, and he was a nice guy.

Once the Eagles' regular season started, they managed a 3-1 start, but then things totally ripped apart at the seams as an 8-game losing streak all but spelled the end of Reid's time in Philadelphia. And so it was with reluctance that I went to see the Eagles play the Bengals on a Thursday night in December with Matt, who is actually a longtime Bengals fan for reasons that I don't think even he completely understands. We had gotten tickets to the game back in the summer, but my enthusiasm for it took a nosedive as the trainwreck of a season wore on. Finally, gameday arrived and I was off to see the 4-9 Eagles go through the motions.

Of course we got there early to tailgate, and so we had already been drinking and standing outside in December weather for over three hours by the time the game even started. The Eagles held the lead in a low-scoring affair late into the third quarter before the Bengals blew their doors off with 24 points in the span of just 3:23 of game time thanks to three consecutive Eagles fumbles. The game had been far from exciting even before then, but the pathetic display by the Eagles only served to make me and the rest of the home crowd understandably quiet and apathetic except for the one guy who kept slamming the back of his boot into the steel-plated stairs. It was simply too cold to cheer and clap, and there wasn't any reason to do so anyway.

As I left the stadium, tired and dissatisfied, my joints felt like they were made of glass. I am pretty sure I can pinpoint this exact moment as when I officially turned into an old man. The whole night reminded me how much better football is on television than in person, and I told myself that I didn't need to attend an Eagles game for a long time after sitting through this one instead of being warm on my couch and able to turn it off after Cincinnati made it a rout. The Eagles wouldn't win another game that year, finishing 4-12, and the axe finally fell on Andy

Reid. Next up: Chip Kelly, the coach whose exciting brand of football would finally deliver a Super Bowl to town. Expectations for Kelly were immediately pushed sky high, and I got to see his first public appearance as Eagles coach at that year's Wing Bowl, though I didn't hear a single word he said because our seats were behind the stage, and WIP or whoever was in charge of the sound system decided that large sections of the Wells Fargo Center didn't need speakers.

That year the Flyers' season didn't even get underway until January thanks to more labor strife courtesy of Gary Bettman and the rest of the stooges in charge of the NHL. The Flyers hit the snooze alarm for the resulting 48-game season, losing six of their first eight games right out of the gate and never recovering as they missed the playoffs for just the second time since 1994. The Sixers had a bad year by any standards, but especially when you consider that prized offseason acquisition Andrew Bynum never suited up for the team. He was a talented player, no question, but the Sixers were only able to get their hands on him because of his health concerns, which of course came to the forefront immediately as he began to experience knee problems.

What followed over the entire season was a comedy of errors, with the team subsequently lying and making excuses about a player who clearly had no desire to do anything but sit back and collect his money. Bynum further aggravated his injury while bowling, doing everything in his power to cement himself as one of the biggest stiffs to ever come to town. Coach Doug Collins also made a plea to the fans to pray for Bynum. It was ridiculous. Following this disaster of a season, the Sixers made big changes. They hired Brett Brown as their head coach and installed Sam Hinkie as general manager. The process had begun.

Unbelievably enough, basketball did bring me a great deal of excitement that spring as La Salle's men's basketball team made their first NCAA tournament appearance since 1992. The team had ranged from bad to mediocre during the years that I had spent there, but now here they were, seven years after I graduated, taking part in March Madness. Well, they weren't in the clear just yet. Because nothing that the NCAA does makes sense, La Salle had a "play-in game" with Boise State, with the winner becoming the #13 seed in the West Region, even though most of the other #14, #15 and #16 seeds were planted in their matchups without having to "earn" their spot like La Salle was going to have to do. Whatever, NCAA. I'm sure their answer to any question is "money", so I'm not even going to bother complaining any more about it.

The Explorers scored an 80-71 win in the game, and I couldn't believe that I actually sat down to watch an entire basketball game on television. The excitement ratcheted up a few days later as La Salle absolutely shocked Kansas State, and March Madness was officially on. The next opponent on the docket was the University of Mississippi, also known as Ole Miss because I guess they hate the actual name of their school. They too fell to the valiant Explorers, and an improbable Sweet 16 berth was the result.

But the proverbial clock struck midnight against Wichita State, and La Salle's amazing run came to an end. I felt immense pride that my school had been able to succeed on the national stage after years of living in the shadow of the rest of the city's teams, most especially Villanova and St. Joe's. La Salle isn't too much smaller than either of those schools, but the gap in their athletic achievements has always been sizable. The Explorers' tournament run represented the most success that any team had in Philadelphia that year, which was cool but also a really depressing commentary on how crappy a year it had been across the board.

The 2013 Phillies season marked the end of the three-year ticket plan arrangement between me and Rich, due in part to the fact that the games were now easier to get tickets to but not entirely discounting the whole Madson/bobblehead fiasco. Yes, the bitterness lingers. And I just didn't feel like being locked into tickets to certain games anymore with the team clearly on the decline. What we didn't expect were for things to be as bad as they were, as the Phils posted just 73 wins, their worst total since Terry Francona's swansong as manager in 2000. Pretty soon and there were going to be free ticket coupons in Phillies franks packages again.

In mid-August, all of my closest friends joined me for a game against the Dodgers as part of my bachelor party. I had always intended on going to either a Phillies or Flyers game to mark the occasion, depending on what time of year my wedding was going to be. But as it turned out, even with the wedding slated for hockey season, it was just easier and more cost-effective to go to a Phillies game a few months before the date. And so we started the festivities by checking in to our hotel and having a few drinks. This was followed by more drinks at Xfinity Live! and then at the game itself. The Phillies, languishing well below .500, had finally pulled the plug on Charlie Manuel earlier that day, ending the most successful managerial run in the club's history. It was not the ideal situation for new skipper Ryne Sandberg to take over, but I had been talking him up for quite a while and was excited about what he could do for the team. His first game behind the bench, however, not so much.

At least I got a solid pitching matchup for my bachelor party as Cliff Lee faced the Dodgers' Zack Greinke. But the Phils' popgun offense managed just three hits in a 4-0 loss. While I was hardly devastated due to the degree of inebriation I was experiencing, I was still bitter that the team had such a pathetic showing on a special occasion for me. Was it too much to ask that the team score a run, let alone win the game? It didn't completely mar my party, but it certainly put me in a bad enough mood to lash out. Again, alcohol.

We returned to the hotel after the game to get ourselves cleaned up before heading back out. Having been fed drinks by my friends all night, I was in a certain condition and simply could not hold back when I saw an older couple wearing Dodgers jerseys in the elevator on the way up to our room. Unprovoked except by the paraphernalia they were wearing, I let loose a string of obscenities at them that I am only aware of because my friends told me after the fact. I hated these people for cheering on the opposition in our park and for "ruining" my bachelor party, then I exclaimed that the Dodgers hadn't won anything in 25 years. And that they sucked, probably with many other words added in there.

I should probably relay to these people somehow that I'm sorry for the way that I acted, but they are most likely dead now so it doesn't matter. It just wasn't my finest moment. Or was it? It was base level, animal instinct fandom on my part, with a sizeable assist from alcohol. Some true passion right there. I was happy to check off "cuss out Dodgers fans in an elevator for no reason" from my Philly sports bucket list, and I should be lauded for it. After even more imbibing, I remember precious little except waking up in the hotel bed at about 4am fully clothed with my shoes on and my contacts still in. Things could have ended way worse, but I have some good friends. They were there for me that night, unlike the Phillies.

The Eagles started their season on fire, building a 33-7 lead over the Redskins on Monday Night Football in Chip Kelly's first game as coach. But they nearly blew it, holding on to win 33-27 after a bad second half of football that was an indicator of things to come. The Eagles lost five of the next seven as their supposedly high-powered offense dried up. Now 3-5 and their season teetering on the edge of disaster, they headed to Oakland for an important game. But I was completely ignoring it because I happened to be getting married that day. Yes, Rachael and I had a Sunday wedding. I know certain types of people would this call a violation, but too damn bad if you have to miss one Eagles game to be with me on the happiest day of my life. Our wedding was planned more than six months before the NFL schedule came out, so they could have adjusted for us.

In a game that I've seen very little of to this day, Nick Foles tied an NFL record with seven touchdown passes in a season-salvaging win. I probably had more than a few wedding attendees irked that they missed such an historical performance, but again, too bad. The Eagles then managed to rattle off three more wins to push their record to 7-5 heading into a pivotal home game against the Lions. With snow in the forecast, the game was going to be heavily affected by the weather, and LeSean McCoy was up to the task. He set a franchise record with 217 yards rushing, and the Eagles got a clutch 34-20 win. This game was awesome to watch because of the visuals provided by the snow on the field and McCoy churning through and around Detroit defenders, kicking up clouds of white that Louis Armstrong would be proud of.

On this particular day, I also discovered the best possible way to watch an NFL game: skip the first half. You see, at this point I was working an overnight shift, so it was largely a necessity to snooze past the 1pm kickoff time. I got home from work about 9:30am and then hit the pillow hard, cramming in five hours or so of sleep before waking up in the third quarter. Detroit had just taken a 14-0 lead and I was immediately regretting my decision to get up, although I did have some shoveling to do before it got dark in a scant few hours. Thankfully, McCoy and the Eagles came alive to validate my viewership, and so I came to the realization that the first halves of NFL games truly don't mean a thing.

If the first half of a game yields a close score, then you will happily watch the remaining thirty minutes (or more) of football and likely forget any storylines or specific plays from the first half. Most games truly can go either way come the start of the third quarter, and so you rarely miss anything big if you don't see the first half for one reason or another. When's the last time your team had a huge win and you were all jacked up on some play from the first quarter? Yeah, I didn't think so. On the other hand, you do get the occasional first half blowout. Yes, you obviously will have missed some game-defining plays if you didn't see it, but was it ever really a game in the first place if it's 31-0 at the break? You can do a quick score check and then maybe do something productive like enjoy your family or go outside during the remaining two hours you would have otherwise spent watching a game that was already decided.

I don't claim that the theory is foolproof because there is the rare epic comeback, but you're allowed to tune back in if things get tight. And you'll already be there for 99% of great finishes to begin with, which is pretty good. This is especially useful for people who do crazy shiftwork, for whom sleep is at a premium. Believe me, it isn't fun to begin with when you wake up in the daytime and know that you won't be able to hit the sack again until the next morning, so it is tough to justify severely cutting into your sleep to watch a whole football game. In the case of this snow game, I found the exact sweet spot, and I was pumped about it. All this being said, it is understood that you will attempt to watch the first half of a game if there aren't extenuating circumstances like the ones I mentioned. And if it's my wedding day, too bad.

The Eagles finished that season 10-6 to win the division and draw a tough match (I sound like a broken record by now) with the Saints in the first round. But the Birds were at home, so the expectations were there. The Eagles led 7-6 after a first half that nobody can remember anything about. See! I told you not to watch! They then surrendered two New Orleans touchdowns to dig themselves a 20-7 hole. But a stirring comeback put them on top 24-23 with 4:54 to play. Predictably, though, it would not hold up against Drew Brees and the Saints' offense. A good kickoff return by future Eagle Darren Sproles coupled with a horse collar tackle at the end of the play put the ball in Eagles territory to begin the drive. At least it looked like the Eagles would get the ball back with plenty of time even if the Saints scored.

Yet the Saints churned out a grueling 10-play drive that only netted 34 yards but effectively crushed the souls of the Eagles' defense and all the fans in attendance. They kicked a field goal at the buzzer to win it 26-24, and that was that. Chip Kelly's first season went out with a whimper, his overworked defense unable to get themselves off the field to give the offense one last shot. An entire season's worth of ridiculously lopsided time of possession numbers had finally bit the team in the butt when it hurt the most.

With the football team falling victim to another first round ouster and the Sixers posting a gruesome 19-63 record and plummeting into obscurity while Sam Hinkie worked his magic, the Flyers had a shot to step back into the limelight. Their entire 2013-14 season was a big "will they or won't they" for playoff positioning that came down to the final games. I found myself back in

Boston in early April as Rachael and I took our first big post-honeymoon trip together. It was her first time in the city, and the schedule had broken perfectly to allow us to take in a late season Flyers-Bruins game followed by an early season Red Sox game two nights later. The Flyers game did not go as planned, as we walked out of a Saturday matinee on the short end of a 5-2 score. That loss would kick off a string of bad luck that Rachael and I had with the Flyers on the road. In less than two years we would see them lose to the Bruins, Islanders, Devils and Capitals by an aggregate score of 20-10. Plus I went all the way to Buffalo with Matt only to see the Flyers lose to the Sabres. I guess I should just stop going to away games.

Despite this setback, the Flyers did enough down the stretch to make the playoffs after a one-year absence from it. And for the first time since 1995, they would meet the Rangers in the postseason. Rachael was slowly but surely checking the boxes as a Flyers fan, so I figured this would be as good a time as any to finally take her to a playoff game. With the Flyers down 2-1 in the series, we headed to the city for Game 4. But first we got some food at South Street and I accomplished one of my own long-time goals by eating an entire "Philly taco". In case you weren't aware, it's a Jim's cheesesteak wrapped in a huge slice of Lorenzo's pizza. I lived to tell the tale and wasn't hungry again for about 20 hours.

As for the game itself, the atmosphere was electric. Not only was it Rachael's first taste of playoff hockey in person, but it was the first playoff game for me since the 2010 Cup Final. All of my pent up energy made me feel like an excited kid as Steve Mason stood on his head to help the Flyers to a 2-1 win, evening the series. Immediately after the exhilarating win, I witnessed a great moment as we entered the concourse and saw throngs of Flyers fans hurling abuse at a small group of cowering Rangers fans, including a young woman. I think that Rachael also joined in the yelling, but I just watched and beamed with pride. It was vintage Philadelphia, and thankfully they held back enough to keep all the Rangers fans out of the hospital, otherwise we'd hear about it forever.

The Flyers won that battle, but New York would ultimately win the war in a seven-game affair where the teams alternated wins. The Flyers had finished two points back of the Rangers during the regular season, and the home ice advantage was ultimately the difference as they dropped three of the four games at MSG in the series. I can't say that the result surprised me, but you do risk getting hurt as a fan any time you put your enthusiasm into something like we had done only to fall short, especially when it's against one of your team's biggest rivals. The Rangers would go all the way to the Stanley Cup Final before they were stopped by the Kings. Thank you, LA, both for this and for beating the Devils two years prior.

When you really hate a team, it hurts your soul to see them win, even more than it pains you to see your own favorite team lose. Does that make any sense? I think I just subscribe to the mentality that if I can't be happy, I don't want anyone else to be either, at least when it comes to sports. At any rate, I was content outside of the sports realm, still newly married and enjoying everything about it. And it was a good time to cling to the positives in my personal and private life even more than ever before, because the Philadelphia sports scene quickly morphed into a barren wasteland.

*

10.

AIN'T NOBODY GOT TIME FOR THAT

Although Rachael and I entered the bonds of holy matrimony and would adhere to the "two people become one" concept that it entailed, this vow did not apply to all of our leanings in sports. As has been mentioned, I managed to flip the hockey switch to turn her from indifferent into a fervent Flyers fan. And while I would continue to support the Sixers and want the best for them, I did not put forth any effort to make it a shared interest of ours, so Rachael remains apathetic about them and the sport of basketball to this day. But as for baseball and football, we would continue to be worlds apart about how to handle those disagreements in our marriage. True, there are worse things to be divided about, but it still posed a conundrum.

While I would carry the flag for the Eagles and Phillies for the entirety of my days for better or worse, Rachael would not drop her support of the Steelers and Braves. The Steelers thing I understand. Her father is from that area and grew up a fan, and then Rachael herself went to Pitt and was exposed to all of that for several years herself. Never mind that I tried to explain to her that Steelers fans are the same people who root for the Penguins, who she out and out despises like I do. She wouldn't budge on it. And since the Steelers have been perhaps the most successful franchise in NFL history, it would seemingly be foolish to jump ship to the Eagles or almost anyone else.

I do take issue, however, with her Braves leanings. As I've explained to people time and time again, she was brainwashed by their prevalence on TBS as she was growing up, and it certainly helped that the Braves were a perennial playoff team. And so I have had to endure an unfortunate number of tomahawk chops in our house and my life in general for a decade now. I can't get her to give the Braves up either, but at least she acknowledges how serious I am about the Phillies, which compelled her to do things early on in our relationship like score me those World Series parade tickets. At this point, I don't think she wishes the team as much ill will as she once did because she sees how much it disappoints me when they suck.

The 2014 Phillies were a good case in point. Their downward slide continued with a 73-89 season where I only bothered to attend one game, which was ironically enough a 1-0 win over the Braves. Ryne Sandberg appeared to be getting next to nothing out of his players, but he was also saddled with the sad remnants of the 2008 team, with only Cole Hamels still performing at a top level. Even then, he got no support from his offense and managed only a 9-9 record on the season despite a career-best 2.46 ERA. And now a quick word about Hamels. Or, I should say, a few quick words. Hall of Fame. He's going. And it is highly likely that he will be the only member of that 2008 Phillies squad to do so. I personally still like Jimmy Rollins to get the call as well because he stacks up very favorably with someone like Barry Larkin who is already in, but if I had to pick just one player from the 2008 team it'd be Hamels.

Cole Hamels fought off the injury concerns and potential character issues that popped up at the beginning of his career to establish himself as one of the best left-handers in baseball for a solid decade. He's a World Series champion and MVP and has a fair number of all-star selections to his name. The no-hitter that he would throw in 2015 was a beautifully crazy way to end his Phillies career before they traded him to the Rangers, and this achievement may be key in his Hall candidacy. But mostly, if health stays on his side, he will be able to pile up so many raw numbers that his case cannot be ignored.

In an era where nobody gets to 300 wins anymore, the new benchmark of 200 career victories are within reach for him. And though that number can be impacted by having a lousy team around you (see: Phillies 2012-2015), Hamels' strikeout numbers are all him. He should be good to hit 3,000 for his career, which would make him a no-doubter in my book. The Hall loves them some strikeouts, and in fact the only hurlers with 3,000 career K's that haven't been inducted are Roger Clemens and Curt Schilling.

There are now more strikeouts than ever happening in baseball, so the club could grow considerably in the years to come. But I think Hamels is far enough ahead of the curve that he will be able to get into Cooperstown before anyone seemingly undeserving of the Hall of Fame puts themselves into the conversation purely based on a high career strikeout total. But anyway, book it for July 28, 2030, because Cole Hamels is headed to the Hall with a Phillies cap perched atop his pretty head.

In the fall of 2014, the Flyers embarked on their first full season with Craig Berube as their head coach. It was an unmitigated disaster. They lost eleven games in the shootout and seven more in overtime to lead the league in the dreaded "OL" or "OTL" category, which I would call surprising, but it wasn't. On the plus side, Jakub Voracek had a nice season and led the team in scoring, ending Claude Giroux's streak of four straight years in that department. But Giroux really needs to be the offensive engine that makes the team go, so his departure from the top spot was bad news. The offense as a whole simply wasn't good enough either. And even though Steve Mason produced a fine season in net, his record ended at an icky 18-18-11 thanks to some horrible overtime/shootout luck. Throw in Ray Emery's subpar season backing him up, and it all added up to the Flyers handily missing the playoffs by 14 points, the second-biggest margin in team history after that 2006-07 season when they came really close but only got nudged out by 36 points. Needless to say, after the season, Craig Berube was not invited back. It was a move that came about four months too late.

But the Flyers looked like the '27 Yankees compared to the 76ers that season, a team that lost its first 17 games of the year and looked to be primed to challenge the NBA's single-season loss record for a time. But they managed to put together four different 2-game winning streaks during the year (nothing longer than that) and finish at 18-64, well clear of the record for futility. And of course their top pick Joel Embiid didn't play all season. Or the next season. Good times.

Because the Eagles' first round playoff loss after the 2013 season clearly showed that Chip Kelly knew what he was doing, it made all the sense in the world for the team to release receiver DeSean Jackson after the best season of his career, letting him go to division rival Washington for nothing. Despite this blow to the team's offense, however, the Eagles still found themselves entering December with an impressive 9-3 record. This included a sterling 6-0 mark at home, with the final two home games of the year up next on the docket. The Eagles had a chance to reclaim the division title and maybe even shore up a first-round bye or get home-field advantage in the NFC. The possibilities were seemingly endless.

But things came to a screeching halt as the Eagles dropped consecutive home games to Seattle and Dallas. They then went on the road and lost to the 3-11 Redskins, with Jackson exacting revenge on the team that cut him by posting a game-high 126 yards receiving. It was all too predictable, and the three straight defeats turned a promising season into a huge missed opportunity. At 9-6, the Eagles were already mathematically eliminated from playoff contention before the season's final week. From Super Bowl dreams before the Seattle game on December 7 to no playoffs after the Washington game on December 20, it took less than two weeks for everything to come crashing down. Unbelievable.

And you can probably guess that Chip Kelly got the squad fired up enough to go out and win a totally meaningless game against the Giants the following week. It was another 10-6 season in the books for Chip. Looked good on paper, but this one was a huge tease, especially when you consider that a team like Carolina won their crappy division and qualified for the playoffs with a record of 7-8-1. In the offseason, Chip asserted his dominance even more. He won a front-office power struggle and shipped star RB LeSean McCoy out of town in a pointless trade with Buffalo. Jeff Lurie and the Eagles were scared that they might lose this gem of a coach if they didn't give him exactly what he wanted. What could possibly go wrong?

Speaking of things going wrong, the 2015 Phils were about to hit absolute rock bottom. With the team 14 games back before the end of June and sporting a hideous 26-48 record, Ryne Sandberg up and quit the team. Nobody was sad to see him go because the situation clearly wasn't working, but nevertheless it was annoying. I had high hopes for this guy and thought that he had navigated his way to the job the proper way and could lead them out of the darkness. Yes, it was going to be rough at first, but I accepted the fact that it would take some time. Instead, he lasted less than two calendar years before simply giving up. Along the way, he was dull as dishwater and didn't provide any real reasons for optimism. A true disappointment indeed. In fact, I had half a mind to include him on my Disliked Athletes list (he did play 13 games for the Phillies in 1981 before the infamous trade to the Cubs), but ultimately decided against it.

Pete Mackanin took over as skipper and did as well as could be expected given what he had to work with. And during the second half of the season, several things occurred that offered hope for the future in various forms. Top pitching prospect Aaron Nola made his big league debut and enigmatic center fielder Odubel Herrera had a solid rookie year from start to finish. I attended one home game on the season (for the second straight year) and the Phillies actually won it! The team traded Hamels to restock the farm system, which was the right move. And they also rid themselves of the malignant Jonathan Papelbon by sending him to the Nationals, whose season hilariously went down in flames as a direct result of the trade. It was really the highlight of the 2015 MLB season. The Phillies shed further dead weight by finally cutting the cord on terrible relief pitcher Phillippe Aumont, and the biggest move of all came in mid-September when Ruben Amaro Jr. was given his walking papers. Yes, the team ended up losing 99 games, but things were at least looking up. They had to at this point.

Entering his third season as Eagles coach and with full control over the personnel and direction of the team, Chip Kelly stumbled out of the gate. The opener was a painful 26-24 Monday night loss in Atlanta, which was even worse for me personally because I had a tonsillectomy and septoplasty earlier that day and watched the game while recovering in the hospital. When I had scheduled the surgery months prior, I didn't give a thought to it conflicting with the Eagles' first game. And so there I was alone, my sinuses packed with gauze and in extreme discomfort, watching the Eagles blow it as I spent the night in the hospital for the first time in my adult life. A win sure would have been nice, but the Birds let me down as I wallowed in misery for a fitful night of barely any sleep.

After dropping the next game to fall to 0-2, the Eagles turned it around and pushed their record to 3-3. They lost to Carolina to head into the bye week below .500, but then scored a critical OT win in Dallas. Any notion that momentum means anything in sports was then quickly disproved as the Eagles dropped a squeaker to Miami and then endured successive blowouts by Tampa Bay and Detroit, the latter coming on Thanksgiving Day and making things absolutely miserable for everyone around here. In true Chip Kelly fashion, when you only deliver wins when it doesn't matter, the Eagles defeated the Patriots in New England to stay alive at 5-7. Next they defeated Buffalo, but it only delayed the inevitable, as they were spanked twice more to drop to 6-9, long gone from any kind of playoff contention.

At this point, Jeffrey Lurie had finally seen enough and canned Chip, ending the experiment long after it had been conclusively proven that the guy was simply not an NFL head coach. But that didn't stop the 49ers from giving him a shot the next season. After posting a 2-14 record, they finally caught on and showed him the door as well. As for the Eagles, after Kelly's firing they went out and won a meaningless final game that season (of course they did) to finish 7-9 when losing it would have meant a higher draft pick and more favorable schedule the next season. But this team is the gold standard, so 6-10 just wouldn't have been acceptable I guess.

In the middle of all the bad headlines the Eagles were creating that season, I received some wonderful news on a personal level that Rachael and I were expecting our first child. Boy or girl, I was excited to be a father and couldn't wait to take them to games and share the overall wonder of sports with them. It would be a few years before they caught on to how miserable sports frequently made me, but I would deal with that at a later time. For now, I was just looking forward to adding another fan to the ranks. And not a minute too soon, because the Eagles and all the other teams in town were killing their loyal fan base with their putrid play and lack of results.

If the Sixers weren't dead to me already, they completely fell off the map with a ludicrously bad 10-72 season, just one game off the worst record in NBA history. They suffered through four losing streaks of at least 12 games and never won two in a row. It was, simply put, an embarrassing display by a team that didn't deserve to be in the league that season. With just a few games to go, Sam Hinkie, architect of the great process that would restore the franchise to its former glory, quit as the team's GM. Some of his many moves would no doubt yield fruit down the line, but the results during his actual tenure at the helm were historically bad.

In the aftermath of his time with the team, some looked upon him favorably for setting them up for success even though he knew he wouldn't be around to see it, like some basketball martyr sacrificing himself for the good of all. I just laugh at him in disdain. The guy was smart and knew what he was doing, but turning the team into an abject mess in order to create the possibility of future success was a slap in the face to anyone who cared about the team and the city.

But there was an actual good basketball team in town that year in the form of the Villanova Wildcats. The program had risen to prominence under Jay Wright but still hadn't gotten over the hump, always seeming to get tripped up early in the tournament despite earning high seeds every year. In March of 2016 they started strong and weren't even challenged in their first three tournament games before a showdown with top-seeded Kansas. The Wildcats netted a 5-point win before completely obliterating Oklahoma in the Final Four to set up a title match with North Carolina. I wasn't exactly hanging on every moment like I was with La Salle's crazy run three years earlier, and in fact I'd be lying if I said I watched any of the championship game. I had actually forgotten it was happening and only flipped over after a breaking news alert scrolled across the bottom of whatever channel I did have on at that time.

So I missed the crazy ending and the shining moment for Philadelphia's newest "champion", but I didn't feel bad about it. I know several Villanova people and I was happy for them. And if someone wants to celebrate a local team winning, that's great and all. But this win was rather localized to me, small potatoes compared to one of our professional teams bringing home an all-too-infrequent title. Villanova's championship was a nice little oasis in the desert, but they could win ten in a row and it still wouldn't fix the Philly sports landscape as far as I was concerned. I still needed to see positive progress from someone at the big league level.

The Flyers were under new management for the 2015-16 season, with fresh-faced coach Dave Hakstol taking over, hired by Ron Hextall solely because of their similar names I'm sure. Seriously, nobody had heard of the guy. The team seemed to alternate wins and losses for a while before a surge in the second half of the season pushed them into the playoff chase. As the season came down to its final games, sad news broke that Ed Snider, the man who literally created the Flyers, was in poor health. The Flyers entered the regular season's final weekend with their status still in doubt, but were able to secure a playoff spot and set up a first round matchup with the league-leading Capitals. It was going to be a tall task for sure, but Flyers fans were relieved just to return to the postseason after missing the previous year, and more importantly were happy for Mr. Snider that he could see the team pull together and make it.

He would pass away on the day following the regular season, at which point a flood of fitting tributes poured in. Though many might disagree with decisions he made over the years, his desire to win and the love he had for the organization and the fans that supported it knew no bounds. His influence on the team and the sports landscape of Philadelphia could never be overstated. The NHL held a moment of silence for him before the playoff openers around the league, and of course during the one in Pittsburgh, someone yelled "Flyers suck!" Classy people out there.

By the time the Flyers kicked off their series, they looked spent. The physical and emotional grind just to make the playoffs had clearly taken a toll, and they managed just 19 shots in dropping the opening game 2-0. Then with the Flyers down 1-0 in the second period of Game 2, Steve Mason allowed possibly the worst goal in NHL history. By now, everyone has probably seen the puck coast from the other end of the ice and slide slowly between his pads. And unfortunately for Mason, it will be the first thing to come up on every Google and YouTube search for the rest of his life unless he manages to cure cancer. Watching it live, I was rendered speechless and bewildered. After something like that, your chances of winning a game drop to pretty much absolute zero. To the Flyers' credit, they did score the next goal, but that would be it as they lost 4-1. Now down two games to none, they were at least returning home for what was sure to be an emotional night.

The Flyers have always done ceremonies and special occasions very well, and their tribute to Ed Snider before Game 3 was no exception. But the moment of silence was a harbinger of things to come that night, as a few drunk and disorderly fans took a cue from Pittsburgh and yelled some stupid and ill-timed things. Once the game actually started, Michael Raffl electrified the building by opening the scoring in the first minute of play. Little did we know at that moment that it would be the only highlight the night would have to offer. Washington tied the game later in the period and they tallied the only goal of the second to carry a 2-1 lead into the third. It felt like the kind of setup that just begged for a comeback, with the home team reaching all the way down for their fans and their late owner to overcome the odds against a superior foe. What we got instead was the most embarrassing period of hockey in franchise history.

Washington started the period on the power play, cashing in at 1:37 to widen their lead. This game was not supposed to be getting away from us like this. Several minutes later, on another power play, they made it 4-1. I felt in my bones going into this series that if the Flyers had one win in them, it would be Game 3, what with the wave of emotion that was sure to be rolling through the building. But by the third period of this game, the Flyers were utterly exhausted and being taken to school by a much better team. Any effort that may have been there sure wasn't showing. They found themselves killing off a five-minute major and surrendered another goal. The fans had had enough. The ones who weren't already streaming for the exits decided to take off the light-up bracelets that had been given out at the door that night and hurl them onto the ice, resulting in a rare delay of game penalty for the home team.

Flyers PA announcer Lou Nolan, in a totally justified display of disgust, told the fans to knock it off and added a sarcastic "way to go" for costing the team and making a mockery of everything. When the humiliation finally came to an end, the Flyers had lost 6-1 and found themselves down in the all-too-familiar 3-0 hole in the series. If there was any justice in the world, this game would have played out much differently. But this is Philadelphia and nothing nice can ever happen, so we suffered a thorough beatdown, both on the ice and from media pundits everywhere who broke out the "batteries and Santa Claus" crap about the fans that we always get so defensive about. If I was ever going to quit being a fan, this would have been the time to do it, owing to how overmatched the Flyers looked in a big spot and the despicable, Pittsburgh-like behavior of many of my fellow fans. But I would stick it out because there was only one more loss to absorb before the season mercifully concluded.

With absolutely nothing to lose, the Flyers turned to Michal Neuvirth in net, sending the battered Steve Mason to the bench. Neuvirth was nothing less than spectacular, turning aside 75 of the 76 shots he faced over the next two games to breathe life into the team and incredibly keep the Flyers in the series. Game 6 saw more of the same, with Neuvirth stopping 28 of 29 shots. But the one that did get by proved to be enough as the Flyers lost 1-0 to drop the series 4-2. They had scored six total goals in the series and were completely overmatched despite the final result getting a little too close for the Caps' liking. Washington would suffer their traditional series loss to the Penguins in the next round, and Pittsburgh won the Stanley Cup a month later. Title #2 for Crosby and company.

Despite all this, the brief foray into the postseason should have served as a painful yet valuable learning experience for the Flyers, a young team hopefully building to something meaningful. They had at least made the playoffs, which not many were expecting. Time would tell if it was the first step on the road to success or just an anomaly for a franchise spinning its wheels and looking for direction.

The Eagles found a new direction at just this time, orchestrating a series of deals to climb all the way up to the second pick in the draft. Howie Roseman, back in power after the Chip Kelly fiasco, took advantage of the hapless Browns to get the guy the Eagles wanted all along, quarterback Carson Wentz. The knock on Wentz was twofold: he had missed time in college with an injury, and when he did play it wasn't against the best competition. Still, everyone could see that he possessed the kind of NFL skill set that a desperate franchise was willing to bet on. Maybe the answer had finally been found.

Just as the Flyers were perishing and the Eagles were reloading in the spring of 2016, the Phillies were reborn and looked good into mid-May, cresting at a 24-17 mark a quarter of the way into the season. But that didn't last long, and a seven-game losing streak pushed them under .500 to stay. Two weeks later, they started a new skid, one that would extend to nine games. And it was during this streak at arguably one of the lousiest points in history to ever be a Philadelphia sports fan that I got a wonderful distraction. My son Nolan came into the world, three weeks early and in the middle of the night, but perfect as far as any of us were concerned. My sleepless nights of working weird hours and/or aggravation at my favorite teams were being replaced by the sleepless nights of new parenthood. But I knew that it would be well worth it.

*

11.

PASSING IT ON

The rest of the 2016 Phillies season played out as badly as you would expect, but I was hardly noticing anything as I was up to my neck in fatherhood and all the dirty diapers that came along with it. Nolan was showered early on with all kinds of clothes and toys sporting mommy and daddy's favorite teams, and it sparked quite a debate in the house. Now that we had a living, breathing child, what direction would he take as a sports fan? You have to go back a couple years to sort through things. We all knew that Nolan would be the Flyers' #1 fan, right up to the day that he suited up for them in the NHL. And if he wanted to find his own path as a basketball enthusiast, he was free to do so. It's a fun game to play as a kid, so if it engendered some passion for the Sixers or whoever, so be it. But baseball and football would be the real sticking points.

Before Nolan even existed as a concept and we were talking about our theoretical future children, Rachael and I came to an agreement. And I will talk about my son here specifically as a stand-in for the speculative kid we were discussing at the time. I made a long and forceful case for the Phillies, going back to my grandfather attending games at Shibe Park in the 20's. Nolan would carry the Lagowski family into its second century of supporting the team, for better or worse. At the very least, the early part of his childhood was going to be spent in this area, so his first baseball memories will be at Phillies games. You root for the home team. Case closed. But I did have to make a concession when it came to football.

On paper, it makes sense. The Steelers had simply had more success than the Eagles. So I don't really blame all the frontrunners that live anywhere north and west of Philadelphia for donning black and yellow during football season and reminding us that they like a team from some city they've probably never spent any time in. Rachael was insistent that our kids would be Steelers fans. I understand her feeling the need to establish this connection, but at the same time, I was confident that eventually the Eagles would win out. I am a bigger football fan than Rachael, so by mere attrition I would be able to create a situation where the home team took over for good. And of course it would help if the Eagles could post some great seasons while Nolan was young and somehow supplant the Steelers among the league's elite.

So Nolan would get Steelers gear from his mom's side of the family and Eagles stuff from mine, and he can make a choice down the road. And until his reaches a certain age, he can even legitimately support both teams for the most part. But at some point, a selection will need to be made so that he doesn't incur the wrath of others for playing both sides. While my family does have a long history of supporting the Eagles, it would not be totally heartbreaking to me if he doesn't choose the Birds, at least not as much as a Phillies snub would be. Call me a bad fan I guess, but as I inch toward middle age, I find that I only have so much sports energy to go around. It helps that the seasons are spaced out the way that they are, but several factors are in play that have prevented the Eagles fan in me from taking over completely.

First, every Eagles season since I was young had felt like death by a thousand tiny stab wounds. Whether it's a collapse or an outright terrible team, a year derailed by injuries or a season where a hated rival wins yet another championship, the end of the season was always accompanied by a bitterness and hopelessness that should be a once-in-a-lifetime feeling. Except it would happen every year, and so I'd choose to throw up a protective barrier for fear of experiencing it again. Just shut down emotionally and wait for the next season. Don't read or watch too much to relive the pain.

The main culprit for every Eagles' letdown being so devastating is the ridiculous overexposure of the team in our local media. Save for a brief period last decade when the Phillies were on top of the world, the Eagles have been #1 for a long time in town. And even as an Eagles fan, it is aggravating. The Flyers have to win fifteen games in a row to get so much as a mention in the local sports media. But tune in to any local outlet in early April when all the other teams are actually playing games that count, and the top story will be that Eagles minicamp is just six weeks away. Philadelphia simply talks about and builds up the Eagles too much. Every week you hear the same idiots call the radio station four days after a game and offer insights that hundreds have already given, I'm guessing just so they can show how big a fan they are and how knowledgeable they are about the team. It is mind numbing.

For me personally, it's also been more difficult to fervently follow the Eagles in recent years because of my work schedule. Waking up in time to watch the second halves of games only works for so long before you feel totally removed from the team. I also admit to having slept entirely through some early games after weighing the costs and benefits of doing so.

Primetime games present the opposite issue, where I can see the early portion but then frequently miss the end because of having to go into work at that time. Basically, it's difficult to navigate an NFL season as a fan if you don't have a weekday 9-5 job.

For the last several years, I have looked at the Eagles' schedule immediately after it is released and then set to work on figuring out which games I will be able to see based on my work schedule, which games I WANT to see and will have to take off for, and which I am going to end up outright missing or only seeing part of. If I lose any fan points in your mind for not seeing every single play, surely I have recouped them by the lengths that I go to so that I can at least see SOME of the season. Baseball and hockey seasons are far too long to worry about this kind of thing, but it's a key skill in steering through the 16-game NFL schedule.

The first battle for Nolan's soul came extremely early in his life, as the Eagles and Steelers met in Week 3 of the 2016 NFL season. Since the Eagles were home, I felt pretty confident because the Steelers hadn't won in Philadelphia since 1965. Now, that only spanned eight games, but it sounds pretty impressive, doesn't it? Still, I thought it would be a tight contest, and so we were all totally shocked by the way the Eagles dominated as they shellacked the Steelers 34-3, to the delight of everyone at my house except for Rachael. And so the Eagles had drawn first blood in the struggle for Nolan's support, although he didn't care and won't remember it. It was just something for dad to cling to.

That win put the Eagles at 3-0 and they were looking fantastic behind rookie QB Carson Wentz. But any momentum gained by the convincing victory was completely destroyed by an ill-timed and extremely early bye the following week. Byes are great for a team when they are struggling or have something to work on, or just to give them a well-deserved rest at the season's halfway mark. This, however, was ludicrous. Firing on all cylinders, a week off was the last thing the Eagles needed, and they predictably came out and lost the next two games. They would go 2-2 over their next four games and looked like they could be in the playoff mix at 5-4, but then the bottom fell out and they lost five straight to kill their season and give Nolan his first taste of Eagles disappointment. The first of many, I was sure.

The 5-9 Eagles pulled their typical rally to win the last two games of the year, which did nothing except hurt their draft position as they finished at 7-9 under rookie head coach Doug Pederson. Wentz had looked great early but faded badly as the season went on. However, he still gave the franchise its best hope at the quarterback position since the departure of Donovan McNabb. And if he could just stay healthy, the team would have many competitive years ahead of them.

That fall, the Flyers looked to build on the unexpected playoff appearance that they had made the previous season. Early on, I attended a game against Detroit, which was the first time I had seen the Red Wings in person since Game 1 of the 1997 Cup Final. The Flyers won the game in overtime, and at long last I could say that I had seen them defeat every other team in the league at the Wells Fargo Center. It was a long time coming. In December, Connor McDavid and the Oilers came to town. It was the only game of the season that I specifically targeted and bought tickets for well in advance. And it lived up to my expectations, as the Flyers rallied from a 5-3 third period deficit, scoring the winning goal with less than two minutes to play in a 6-5 victory. It was the team's seventh straight win, a streak that would eventually reach ten games. The team looked primed to take the next step.

But after that point, nothing worked. The goaltending, playing behind a shaky defense, wasn't very good. And the scoring was middle of the pack, with Claude Giroux especially having a bad year by his standards. A couple of bright spots poked through, like the play of rookie defenseman Ivan Provorov, but it wasn't nearly enough to get them close to a playoff spot. I didn't make it back to another game in the season's final four months, which was a real shame considering that the two early games I did get to were great. And once again, the Penguins skated off with the Stanley Cup, their third in less than a decade while the Flyers missed the playoffs for the third time in five seasons. It couldn't get much worse. The year left me feeling down on the team and the direction it was headed.

The Sixers and their fans would finally get their first look at Joel Embiid that season, and he did not disappoint. The team was understandably cautious with his minutes, but he was the talk of the league when he did play. And I actually paid to attend a Sixers game, although it was part of a friend's bachelor party so it's not like it was my idea in the first place. That night, Embiid was scintillating in a win over the Charlotte Hornets, the team whose Starter jacket you had when you were a kid because you thought the colors were cool.

Unfortunately, Embiid's season would come to an early end a few weeks later with another injury. As usual, the team hemmed and hawed about the severity of it before finally shutting him down, lying their way through the last two months of the campaign as they finished with 28 wins. It was their best showing since 2012-13, which is sad, but at least it offered a glimmer of hope. Top overall pick Ben Simmons had missed the entire season with an injury, and the expectation was that he could provide the added boost needed in the following season to get the team back to respectability. In a league where one player can make the difference between a bad team and a playoff squad, the Sixers appeared to have a few game-changers who just needed to stay healthy.

I thought that 2017 would be a transition year for the Phillies, finishing at or just below .500 while making the leap into wild card contender status the next season. The young core was ready to start making an impact, or so I felt. When Rachael visited Las Vegas with her sisters shortly before the season started, my dad and I gave her a chunk of change to place an "over" bet for the Phillies' seemingly modest 73.5 win projection. I honestly didn't understand why the experts had set the number so low. The Phils were coming off a season where absolutely nothing had gone right but they had still managed 71 wins. Surely, they would scoop up at least a handful more this year.

The first game I attended was a late April matinee against the Marlins. The Phillies won 3-2 to push their record to an encouraging 11-9 mark as they shipped out for a bizarre road trip that would take them to Los Angeles and Chicago. It would prove to be a very early undoing to their season. They lost the first game of the trip to the Dodgers, but then were in excellent shape in the second game, leading 5-2 heading into the bottom of the ninth. And so I sat stunned as "closer" Hector Neris gave up home runs to the first three batters he faced to tie the game, with the Dodgers pushing across the winning run later in the inning. Talk about demoralizing. The Phils were now 11-11 and would not get above .500 for the rest of the year. They would go 1-6 on that road trip, and followed it up with a 2-7 trip just a few weeks later. There was another 2-7 road trip in June. You get the picture. They just stunk.

The lone highlight for me personally was when Rachael and I took Nolan to his first ever Phillies game, a Sunday afternoon matchup against the Braves in late July. It was dad's team vs. mom's team, which was fitting. It's almost like I planned it that way. On that day, the Phillies actually came out on top, with Freddy Galvis knocking home the winning run in the bottom of the ninth to give the Phillies a 2-1 win in a game that was, frankly, boring. But I was happy that

Nolan "saw" a win on his first try. I am definitely tempted to never take him again so he can remain undefeated. The lack of excitement aside, it was a dream realized for me to go to a game with my wife and son, even if Nolan crapped himself and had no idea what was going on. It was basically like watching a game with a Mets fan. Still, it was a happy day for me, and Rachael didn't care much about the Braves' loss because they weren't going anywhere either that season.

All of the Phillies' top prospects did bubble up to the big leagues later that year, providing somewhat of a silver lining to the dismal campaign and showing that just maybe there was hope for the future. The highlight was, of course, Rhys Hoskins and his otherworldly home run binge after making his major league debut. Perhaps he could combine with the likes of JP Crawford, Jorge Alfaro, Scott Kingery and Aaron Nola to form the sort of Howard-Rollins-Utley-Hamels core that birthed a champion years before. Time will tell. It's been a while since the team contended, and it's about time they got back to it.

Nolan got to attend his first Flyers game about four months later, which was a proud moment for me. Thankfully we got to sit in a club box courtesy of Rachael's work, because I was not about to hold a wiggling 1-year old on my lap in one of the Wells Fargo Center's ridiculously narrow seats whose unnecessary cup holders dig into your sides and further immobilize you. Anyway, the Flyers were up 3-1 after one period, but ultimately fell 5-4 in overtime to Calgary. Nolan did get to see a hat trick in his first Flyers game, just like his mom did, but it was by an opposing player. One bright spot in the game was rookie Nolan Patrick, who scored his second career goal and first at home in the NHL. First of many hopefully, as his development will be a key determining factor in whether or not this team can contend in the coming years. He'll never be my favorite Nolan, but I'll be watching him closely and rooting for his success.

Shortly before taking Nolan for his first experience of watching the Flyers lose in person, I tasted victory on a personal level. After all the years spent sitting around and absorbing the often painful chatter coming from my radio, I finally decided to call WIP, albeit only to enter their "Beat the Hammer" trivia contest against midday host Joe DeCamara. As luck would have it, I was able to get through at the right time to become the contestant for that week's showdown. With the Phillies' 2017 season coming to an end right around there, the category was appropriately "Phillies Season Endings".

Joe had won 32 of his first 34 matches in the weekly contest, and so the deck was seemingly stacked against me. But I was pretty confident in my Phillies knowledge and thought that I had a shot. By the time the dust had settled, I had surprised myself by answering all four of the questions correctly, the first challenger to accomplish such a feat. It was then up to Joe to match what I had done to force a tiebreaker. After answering the first question correctly, he was unable to name the Phillies' opponent in their final game at the Vet (Braves), and so I had won right then and there, although the contestant's performance is hidden from him until after he has finished his set of questions.

Joe also missed the "trick question" that I had gotten right, which asked "In what four seasons since 1990 have the Phillies played in the last game of the Major League Baseball Season?" The three obvious answers are 1993, 2008 and 2009, years in which they had appeared in the World Series. Taking a stab at the last answer, I had said 1994 because it had been shortened by a players' strike. This turned out to be correct, as researched by WIP producer and question-asker James Seltzer.

And so DeCamara ended up going 2 for 4 and was then told that I had had a perfect round, at which point his co-host, former Eagle Jon Ritchie, ran through the studio yelling exuberantly. I later saw the video online. It was awesome that a former Eagle seemed genuinely excited for me, although I am sure a good deal of his giddiness was in being able to make fun of his co-host. Either way, I had finally established myself as Philadelphia's foremost sports expert. In my mind at least.

As I ascended to my throne, the 2017 Eagles were starting to do something amazing. It certainly looked like a middling year was in the cards for the team, but they had other ideas. I could break it all down in the style that I have employed throughout this book, but it's so fresh in our collective minds that I would be wasting words reminding you of all of the big moments of the season and how the team overcame the adversity brought on by an onslaught of injuries and the naysayers who thought they weren't for real. Plus, if you want a blow-by-blow recap, you can always turn to Ray Didinger or any of the other great writers in this town that can provide it to you. I thought about including a whole chapter covering the 2017 Eagles, wittily titled *Hell Freezes Over* or *The Promised Land* or something like that, but I just didn't feel it necessary. So, here it goes…

The seminal moment of the season would of course come when Carson Wentz suffered a season-ending knee injury, triggering a shock wave of pre-disappointment across the area as we awaited the inevitable failure of a season that had so much promise up to that point. It was the most poorly-timed injury in the history of our teams, but one that sadly wasn't all that surprising. It always happens to us, right? Just when it looked like this could be our year. But the team's confidence in itself never wavered, even if its most ardent fans were ready to jump off the Ben Franklin Bridge.

A 13-3 record set the team up with a first round bye and home field advantage in the conference, but because Nick Foles was under center and nobody in the mainstream media believed in Doug Pederson, they were dubbed home underdogs for their first game against the Falcons. No matter. A 15-10 nail biter of a win followed, which brought to town the Minnesota Vikings, who would be playing the Super Bowl in their home stadium if they could get by the Eagles. This extra motivation was enough for the "experts" to pick against the Eagles again, but they paid it no heed, winning in a 38-7 blowout.

A spark had been ignited in all Eagles fans as our wildest dreams came rising to the surface. The magical run had one last leg, and it would come against Tom Brady and the Patriots, the most challenging of all obstacles. Surprise, surprise, guess who was favored. The two weeks leading up to the game seemed to stretch on forever as everyone waited with baited breath. Finally, on the day of, I took a few moments to write the following…

I'm writing this part on the morning of February 4, 2018. Super Bowl LII between the Eagles and the Patriots is less than ten hours away. By the end of the day, Philadelphia will either be kicking off the most raucous and joyful party it has ever seen or likely be laid to waste by the most disappointed fans to ever populate the earth. There seemingly is no in between.

If they lose, the feeling will be crushing. Like a weight sitting on our collective chests until one of the teams rises up to the level of a champion again. The 2008 Phillies, already deep in our memories, will likely cease existing entirely in our consciousness because any recollection we may have of actually winning will not be fathomable from the pit of despair we will be wallowing in after this game. This Eagles team was not expected to be here, but now that they are, falling just short will be infinitely more painful than having been a nonfactor and finishing 8-8 this season.

If they win…I don't know. I can't wrap my head around it. Elation, amazement, every emotion conceivable and the tears that accompany them will come pouring forth from all Eagles fans. The inferiority we have been made to suffer by fans of the Cowboys, Giants and most of the league at large will end. They will continue to bitterly lord their multiple titles over us in a display of their true colors, but it will no longer have any merit. This one will last a lifetime and we can all go to our graves with that satisfaction. There is no way to play this one safe. It's one extreme or the other. The beauty of sports, and its utter cruelty, will be simultaneously on display tonight. For Philadelphia fans, this is the game we have waited our whole lives for. It's frightening and exhilarating. But we all signed up for it. Here goes nothing.

Well…

OH

MY

GOD

In one for the ages, they did it. Eagles 41, Patriots 33. We will always remember the Philly Special and so many other key plays in the game, culminating with a dejected Tom Brady sulking and leaving the field a loser. He couldn't even be bothered to shake the hand of the man that bested him on the game's ultimate stage. What a baby. Really, I think "greatest game ever" says it all. Party time. And not to look the proverbial gift horse in the mouth, but I wish that Nolan were just a couple years older so that I could have celebrated it with him and achieved the full magnitude of the win. Hopefully this will occur sooner rather than later.

As it was, I got to be with my dad for a game full of thrills and, ultimately, a jubilant moment that will last me for the rest of my life. You all experienced it in your own special way. It was transformative. Nothing will ever be the same again, and I mean that in the best possible of ways. The 2008 Phillies' World Series win will always be so special to me, but even being a bigger overall fan of baseball than football, this Eagles title blew its doors off plain and simple. As the whole of the Delaware Valley let out the most liberating scream of victory in the history of sports, it felt great not to just be a Philadelphia sports fan, but to be alive in general. That's just what sports does. It takes a group of people from all walks of life, diverse in so many ways, and makes them all feel like part of the same family. All because of a silly little game. Amazing.

A few days later came the parade, and while it will go down in history as the city's greatest celebration based on sheer scale alone, Jason Kelce's frenzied and borderline insane speech/tirade was the ultimate capper of a great day and a miracle season. My personal favorite line was "Lane Johnson can't lay off the juice" as Kelce listed all the shortcomings of his teammates, circling around to how the Eagles proved all the critics wrong. The whole thing was a beautifully ridiculous middle finger to the rest of the league. Needless to say, it was brilliant. Sorry, Chase Utley, your speech became a mere footnote. Every Eagles fan got exactly what they needed out of it. The phrase "Super Bowl Champion Philadelphia Eagles" finally started to sink in.

Maybe, just maybe, this championship will be some kind of catalyst to push Philadelphia to the forefront of the national sports scene. We have had our spurts of success before, but if you squint really hard you can see all of our teams being true contenders at the same time very soon, providing this town's fans with a year-round smorgasbord of great players leading their teams to victory. If you check back in a decade, names like Joel Embiid, Aaron Nola, Ivan Provorov, Ben Simmons and Nolan Patrick could be bona fide Philadelphia legends for helping their teams win a championship or two. Or more. Nothing can be classified as a sure thing, but I am feeling good about it. It isn't in the same category as death, taxes and the trumpet player outside the stadiums after the games only knowing how to play the *Rocky* and *Addams Family* themes, but it's close.

After years of expecting the worst, I don't want to get ahead of myself by going in the complete opposite direction, but maybe I'm turning over a new leaf as a fan. This could be the time to stop the negativity and doubting once and for all and to start believing. The "disease of the mind" of being a Philadelphia sports fan looks to have found at least a temporary panacea. All of the irrationality, fears and paranoia that define this sports complex of mine are now alleviated. But give it time and it will return. That's just how it goes. The taste of winning must be followed by even more.

Shortly after the Eagles hoisted the Lombardi Trophy, Villanova's men's basketball team captured their second NCAA title in three seasons. It was a marvelous accomplishment on their part but not a reason to celebrate for me personally. Also in the immediate aftermath of the Eagles winning, the Flyers and 76ers seemed to kick things into high gear with solid stretch drives of their own. The Flyers made the playoffs despite looking very iffy midway through the season, while the Sixers rode the wave of a franchise-record winning streak to their first playoff appearance in six years and made the second round of the postseason. Even the Phillies looked good out of the gate in 2018. Early brain cramps by rookie manager Gabe Kapler provided valuable lessons and the team responded with solid play rather than going off the rails in April, a sight far too common since the end of the team's World Series era. All in all, it seems to be a great time to be a fan in this town.

These teams are a lifetime commitment for me, and hopefully for you as well. Day in and day out, they are there for our investment, which is why we care so much. Their constant presence is a stabilizer in our lives and a rallying point for friends and families. And it feels so good right now. We all chased the dream and caught it. Our goal realized, our faith rewarded, our greatest desires satisfied. What a marvelous feeling. Worth it. Now, let's keep it going.

*

12.

50 MOST DISLIKED PHILADELPHIA ATHLETES

This idea has its genesis in a list that I compiled on my college sports show in 2004. I had heard that the Baltimore Orioles were celebrating their 50th anniversary that year by holding a fan vote for the 50 most popular Orioles ever and then honoring them at a game. I thought to myself, in typically cynical Philadelphia fashion, that I should turn the idea on its head.

The footage of me reciting my list of disliked Philadelphia athletes is unfortunately lost to history, otherwise I would be tempted to just reprint it and give a postmortem evaluation of it all these years later to see who my feelings might have changed about. Instead, I am forced to create a new register of futility, a "dishonor roll" if you will. Armed with an extra decade-plus of players to hate, this will be more fun anyway. I can remember offhand a good number of those unfortunate souls who made the original list and many will still be on this one. And one guy in particular still holds onto the number one spot. I doubt he'll ever move. Any guesses before we get started?

The criteria: These are players who I have personally witnessed playing for Philadelphia teams in my lifetime. They may make this list because they flat out sucked, fell short of expectations, were a-holes or troublemakers off the field, or because they looked at me funny one time. I did take input from a few friends but ultimately this is extremely subjective from person to person, although I hope you will agree with many of the picks.

Finally, keep in mind that I am limiting this to PLAYERS WHO ACTUALLY PLAYED GAMES FOR A PHILADELPHIA TEAM. So JD Drew and Andrew Bynum will not appear. Sorry about your luck. Neither will Chris Wheeler or any media member you may have hated. Not even Terry Francona or any managers/coaches although I despise many of them. Just players. Now, before we get into the list proper, here in alphabetical order are a few notable omissions…

Bobby Abreu – Man, this guy put up some numbers, but Phillies fans will always have this impression of him as a guy who dogged it and could have been even better. As for me, I liked Bobby enough to not consider including him on this list. Beggars can't be choosers when it comes to Phillies that actually had some talent.

Nelson Agholor – Things started off poorly for the Eagles' 2015 first round pick, with just 59 catches, 648 yards and 3 touchdowns total over his first two seasons. He looked ticketed for a prime spot on this list. But he finally proved his worth in 2017 with a solid year as the Birds won the Super Bowl. What a turnaround.

Shawn Andrews – Andrews sure looked like a stud and it seemed the Eagles had hit big on their 2004 first round pick. But after a couple of Pro Bowl selections, Andrews mysteriously left the team during training camp in 2008, citing an ongoing battle with depression. He came back eventually, played two games, but then got hurt and never played another game as an Eagle. A colossal disappointment given the expectations.

Nolan Baumgartner – One of the many crap signings the Flyers made before their ill-fated 2006-07 season was the two-year deal they handed Baumgartner, a classic extra defenseman that they expected something out of for no good reason. After just six games on the team, he got waived. Nobody wanted him so he played for a few months with the Phantoms. After that, who the hell cares?

Roman Cechmanek – Personally I loved this nutty guy, so he was nowhere near my list. I just thought I'd mention him here for those who would disagree. Besides having a cool name and looking like Mr. Bean, Cechmanek put up amazing numbers for the three years he tended the Flyers' goal and won me some money since he was on my fantasy hockey team. It wasn't his fault the team couldn't score.

Alexandre Daigle – A tremendous bust as the NHL's #1 overall pick by Ottawa in 1993 (ahead of Chris Pronger!), Daigle was already a punchline by the time he got to the Flyers. And so you can't say you were all that disappointed by his 31 points in 68 games for the Flyers before he was sent packing again. The biggest source of annoyance here was that the Flyers gave up the promising Vinny Prospal to get Daigle. Wish we had that one back.

Chase Daniel – Serving as a backup QB in New Orleans and Kansas City for the first six years of his pro career, Daniel had thrown a measly 77 passes in the NFL before the Eagles signed him to a 3-year, $21 million contract to back up starter Sam Bradford and possibly even push him for the job. But when Bradford was traded a week before the season, the Eagles (rightly) handed the reins over to rookie Carson Wentz, not even trusting Daniel to keep the seat warm for a few weeks. He threw one pass as an Eagle and was released the following offseason. He didn't even do enough to be disliked, so I couldn't justify putting him on the list.

Brian Dawkins – Kidding. Just making sure you were still paying attention. I really want you to enjoy this.

Lenny Dykstra – You can think whatever you want to about "The Dude". But are you really surprised at the way his post-baseball life has turned out? There's not much need to pile on. The fact that he's so far removed from his time with the Phillies also plays a part in keeping him from the list. The guy was a very productive player, and it's better to just separate all the later stuff from it. Dwelling on it just feels excessive in this case for some reason.

Matt Geiger – Oh, to be seven feet tall. Geiger battled injuries throughout his four seasons with the Sixers, ultimately bilking them out of over $35 million for a mere 154 games played for the team. If I was a bigger basketball guy, this dude would have made the list for certain. As it is, I at least want to make sure that he gets mentioned. He earned it, unlike his money.

Ryan Howard – I include "The Big Piece" here just to address the haters who remember only the overpaid, broken-down Howard from 2012 on. Let's not forget that he AVERAGED 44 home runs and 133 RBI a season over a six-year period. He was probably two seasons like that away from being a slam-dunk first ballot Hall of Famer. All that aside, the man delivered a World Series and was must-see TV for the better part of a decade. You're welcome, Phils fans. If you think he should have been on this list, get the hell out.

Mike Jackson – Jackson pitched with the Phillies in 1986 and 1987, even starting a handful of games. Results were meh. But where he truly merited consideration for this list was his 2000 "season" for the Phillies. Signed to be the team's closer, he got injured warming up in the bullpen during the team's opening series and never appeared in a game, spending the whole year on the DL. $3 million wisely spent by Ed Wade.

Jevon Kearse – The Eagles broke the bank to bring in "The Freak" before the 2004 season. And even though he didn't put up huge numbers, the move looked good as his presence on the team's defense was a key factor as the Eagles reached their first Super Bowl in my lifetime. But as the team regressed in 2005, dissatisfaction started to grow when he wasn't putting up stats in line with his gaudy contract. An injury and a down year later, Kearse lost his job and was cut by the Eagles after the 2007 season. He collected over $29 million for his time in Philly.

Eric Lindros – The younger version of me was so bitter at how the Lindros saga played out that I wished the guy had never played for the Flyers. But I have grown wiser, and just as Lindros and the Flyers have kissed and made up, I resign myself to the fact the he was the greatest Flyer of my lifetime and would reside in the pantheon of all Philadelphia sports if not for the injuries that derailed his time in town. If we could have just gotten a Cup out of all this it would never have been an issue. Lindros has finally been rightly celebrated, but any mention of him will always stir up a sadness inside me over what might have been. At one time he would have been on this list, but at this point I think that everyone has seen the light.

Donovan McNabb – From the booing at the draft through the Super Bowl dry heaves to his unceremonious exit from town, Philly never warmed up to McNabb. But you can't deny his place in Eagles history, and so it is nearly impossible to include him on a list like this unless you are really vindictive. After all, #5 will always love you. The feeling wasn't mutual, but you have to hand it to him for a borderline great Eagles career.

Adam Morgan – First surfacing with the Phillies in 2015, Morgan seemed like the latest in a long line of Matt Beech-type below average pitchers that the organization "developed" just to take up space on the roster. He even posted a 6.04 ERA in 2016. A trip to the bullpen seemed like it did him a lot of good, as he was much better the following year, especially in the second half. But it now seems like that was just an anomaly, and this guy stands as an example of the ineptitude on the mound the team has seen its fair share of for decades.

Terrell Owens – As previously mentioned, the guy was Public Enemy #1 for a time. But blame has to be leveled on all parties involved, and so T.O. escapes the list. I sure wish we had him for a couple more years. Again, his personality does him no favors, but he doesn't "make the cut".

Vicente Padilla – While the "Wolf Pack" and even the "Byrd Cage" were tolerable, I think we can all agree that the "Padilla Flotilla" was the dumbest fan group to ever grace the upper levels of the Vet. But Padilla was just useful enough to avoid this list despite underperforming relative to his level of talent and looking like a 50-year old when he was 25.

Chad Qualls – Qualls stands in as another representative for the myriad horrible relievers the Phils have employed over the last few decades. He didn't do anything outstandingly bad enough to make the main list, but he wasn't good either, compiling a 4.60 ERA over half a season before he was sent packing. I think I'm just bitter about him because he was part of the 2012 team that signaled the Phillies' decline after five years of dominance.

Michael Saunders – He was an all-star in Toronto in 2016 but faded horribly in the second half of that season, so the Phillies were able to sign him on a one-year deal to act as a stopgap in their outfield. With any luck, he would play well enough that they could flip him to a contender at the deadline for some kind of future assets. But he didn't even last three months, as he hit .205 over 61 games and was released. He did net a cool $9 million for his (lack of) efforts though.

Curt Schilling – Schilling is probably one of the top five starting pitchers in Phillies team history, but he didn't endear himself to anyone due to his gruff personality. And while his exit from town wasn't as ugly as that of some other players, he clearly didn't want to be here anymore. It was tough watching him win three World Series elsewhere, and his post-career shenanigans have put a further damper on our image of him.

James Thrash – Two years into the Andy Reid/Donovan McNabb era, it was obvious that the Eagles had something special brewing. So they went out and signed Thrash for some reason, who became the team's de facto #1 receiver. His first year was solid, as he posted 833 yards and eight touchdowns. But by his third year as an Eagle, those numbers had slipped to 558 yards and one measly touchdown. He also repeatedly came up small in the playoffs, which led directly to the Eagles making a move for Terrell Owens. So I guess we owe him a thank you for that. Plus, when he was traded to the Redskins, the Eagles used the pick they received to draft Trent Cole. Thanks again, James!

R.J. Umberger – Umberger's first stint with the Flyers, culminating in a very strong playoff performance in 2008, is the lone saving grace that keeps him from making this list. That offseason, he was traded to Columbus, where he turned into a consistent and durable 20 to 25-goal guy every year. But as his game started to slide, the Flyers reacquired him in 2014 for the popular and still productive Scott Hartnell in a swap that still has people scratching their heads to this day. Once he came back to town, it was immediately apparent that Umberger's best days were behind him. He scored just once in his first 24 games that season, then finished the year off by going scoreless in his final 18 games. A 9-goal, 15-point season while Hartnell put up 28 goals and 60 points for his new team. Umberger followed it up the next year with 2 goals in 39 games, and the Flyers mercifully bought out the final year of his contract. Regrets all around.

Now, the moment you've been waiting for. Here is the official list of my 50 Most Disliked Philadelphia Athletes…

50. Ronnie Brown – Signed before the 2011 season to act as a backup to Shady McCoy, Brown looked totally used up after six seasons of hard running with Miami. After getting just thirteen uninspiring carries through four games, he rode the pine for a pair before the Eagles traded him. But the player coming back in return failed his physical and the trade was voided so Brown, like a chronic skin disorder, was coming back. As the Eagles' season swirled down the drain, he never managed more than eight carries in any game and finished the season with a grand total of 136 yards on 42 carries. He was painful to watch in his lone year as an Eagle but somehow managed to hang around the league until 2014.

49. Omar Daal – Part of the awful haul in the Curt Schilling trade, Daal was 2-10 for Arizona at the time of the deal and then went 2-9 for the Phillies to finish up the 2000 season, leading baseball with 19 losses that year. He was better in 2001 but he'll forever be remembered for his role in such a disappointing period of Phillies baseball. Let him serve as a reminder of how front office failure can enrage a fan base.

48. Cary Williams – Maybe he was just a victim of the Chip Kelly system whereby a defense was exposed by having to spend 40+ minutes per game on the field. At any rate, Williams got picked apart and overmatched by receivers for two seasons before mercifully leaving town. Just another underachieving Eagle in a long line of them.

47. Danny Tartabull – He signed with the Phillies before the 1997 season for $2 million when nobody else would offer him anything near that. In his first at-bat of the season, he fouled a ball off his foot. Playing through it for a couple games, he would go 0 for 7 in his Phillies career before going on the DL, never playing again for the team and ultimately retiring. Seriously. That's real commitment right there, Danny.

46. Freddie Mitchell – FredEx was truly one of the biggest draft disappointments the Eagles have ever had. If not for 4th and 26, he would be even more of a punchline than he already is. The final tally: 4 years as an Eagle, 90 catches for 1263 yards and 5 touchdowns. That's a big whiff from Big Red on a first-round pick.

45. Ricky Watters – He may have the best numbers and the most productive Philadelphia career of anyone on this list. But three borderline great seasons (over 5000 total yards from scrimmage) still were not enough to eclipse Ricky's immortal "For who? For what?" moaned after his first game as an Eagle in reference to why he gave up on a pass over the middle to avoid a potential hit. Ricky was probably right, but he showed us over and over again that he just wasn't Philly enough. And that just won't fly.

44. Chris Gratton – With the team having just fallen short in the 1997 Cup Final, the Flyers went out and signed Gratton, a big powerful center just turning 22 years old who seemed like an ideal fit to provide the kind of secondary scoring that was sorely lacking after Lindros and LeClair. His first (and only) full season as a Flyer was decent, as he matched his career high with 62 points but saw his goal total from the previous year dip from 30 to 22. The following year, he posted a grand total of one goal in 26 games before being drummed out of town and traded back to Tampa from whence he came.

43. Billy Tibbetts – Well, this was a mess. Tibbetts had served 39 months in prison for a statutory rape conviction while in his early 20's. Amazingly he worked his way back into hockey and made the NHL with the Penguins. After parts of two seasons with them (9 points in 62 games), the Flyers inexplicably traded for him. He played 9 games for the orange and black before being released and then appeared with the Rangers for a cup of coffee the following season before his NHL career ended. After his career, he led police on two separate high-speed car chases. Let us never speak of him again. Yuck.

42. Dennis Cook – Cook actually pitched in parts of two seasons as a starter with the Phillies earlier in his career before returning as an elderly left-handed reliever in a trade during the 2001 season and stinking his way to a 5.59 ERA over 19 appearances. He was better than Turk Wendell (7.47 ERA post-trade that year) who came over in the same deal, but at least Wendell would stick in town longer and perform decently.

41. Jiri Dopita – A force in European hockey for a decade, Dopita came to the Flyers in 2001 as "the best player in the world not playing in the NHL yet". He scored 4 goals in one game against the hapless Atlanta Thrashers (RIP), but that shining moment aside, he would total only 27 points in 52 games. Take away the one explosion and he scored 7 goals the rest of the year. Then he hurt his knee, and he was traded after the season. He later played 21 games for Edmonton, and that was it for his NHL career. Thanks for your service, Jiri.

40. Domonic Brown – Brown will forever be synonymous with the phrase "Can you believe this guy made an all-star team?" Indeed he did in 2013, thanks largely to a torrid six-week stretch. But it was a complete and utter mirage. A bust in every sense of the word, the Phillies held onto Brown for years, refusing to trade him when he was highly coveted by many teams. The final play of his Phillies (and maybe MLB) career came when flew into the stands and got hurt while misplaying a blooper down the line into an inside-the-park home run. It was perhaps the most fitting end for any Philadelphia athlete ever, so he's got that going for him at least.

39. Riley Cooper – You could probably scoop a guy off Castor Avenue that would give you the same amount of production that Cooper did over his six (six!) inexplicable seasons as an Eagle. Aside from being a poster child for mediocrity, Cooper made an infamously stupid comment that rightly got him into a lot of trouble. Given his status as entirely replaceable, you'd think the team would have cut ties with him right then and there, but he still stuck around for three more years. You have to wonder what the team was thinking.

38. Bradley Fletcher – Another mistake of a free agent signing and misguided attempt by Chip Kelly to shore up the secondary, Fletcher bungled his way through two seasons as a Bird. He allowed the most passing yards in the league in his first year, then was equally terrible in the second. He was off the team for two years before I realized he was gone; he was just one of those guys whose specter of terribleness makes you forget he's not physically there anymore.

37. Jerome McDougle – The Eagles traded up in the 2003 draft to select McDougle, a promising defensive end, in the first round. Hopes were high. And after two unimpressive seasons to start his career, there were still expectations. But those were all but extinguished when McDougle was shot during the 2005 offseason and missed the entire year. He returned the next season to little effect, then missed all of 2007 with another injury. His grand totals as an Eagle: 33 games played over five seasons, three sacks. Way to go.

36. Ulf Samuelsson – Samuelsson took the normal stereotype of the smooth-skating, finesse Swedish defenseman and turned it on its head. An utterly detestable cheap-shot artist, Ulfie was loathed by Flyers fans who watched him for years during his stints with the Penguins and

Rangers. So one has to wonder why the Flyers signed him in 1999 other than to put the old "You hate a guy unless he's on your team" saying to the ultimate test. Well, we still hated him. Ulf played out the string and then retired after his lone season as a Flyer. Good riddance.

35. Jose Mesa – Joe Table enjoyed two good seasons to start his Phillies tenure, nailing down saves for a seemingly up-and-coming team. But any hope for 2003 left the station when it was Jose Mesa time, as he compiled a hideous 6.52 ERA across 61 games before leaving as a free agent. Yet the Phillies decided they wanted more and brought him back four years later following his release by the Tigers, where he had posted a 12.34 ERA through his first 16 appearances that season. He got into 40 games for the Phillies, put up a 5.54 ERA in low leverage situations, then finally retired.

34. Matt Read – After his first two seasons in the NHL, Read looked like a decent contributor for a Flyers team that seemingly was always lacking depth scoring from the wings. He didn't fit the typical Flyers "big tough guy" mold, but he had speed, a good shot and wasn't afraid to play physically despite his smaller frame. And then the wheels fell off, as Read became a total nonfactor and posted successive seasons of just 8, 11, and 10 goals. He then registered a single goal over 19 games in his final season as a Flyer after spending most of the year in the minors. All the while, everyone wondered what a replacement-level guy like this was doing jamming up a roster spot. Is it fair to single out a third-line player and put him on a list like this? Probably not, but he fits the criteria and just became painful to watch.

33. LJ Smith – For four years, Smith was a consistent offensive threat from the tight end position, but we all still held out hope for a truly big breakout from him. He had the size and the ability, but the sum of the parts just didn't add up. Nagging injuries seemed to constantly affect his play, and his ball control was atrocious. After making a catch, he'd run with it like a loaf of bread, just inviting defenders to take it. His promise went ultimately unfulfilled and he left the Eagles after six seasons. A 2-catch campaign in Baltimore was his last NFL action, and he was out of the league before his 30th birthday.

32. Jeff Hackett – The Flyers signed a 35-year old Hackett to be their starting goalie prior to the 2003-04 season. The deal certainly seemed like a Band-Aid move until something better came along, but Hackett made a strong first impression by registering shutouts in his first two games with the team. However, things started going way downhill in mid-December, and he lost nine out of ten starts. Something was wrong. It would turn out to be the end of his NHL career, as he was diagnosed with vertigo and retired after playing just 27 games as a Flyer. Only in Philadelphia.

31. Jerome Williams – Williams had a good enough showing for the Phils at the end of the 2014 season to earn himself a contract for 2015. But then he muddled his way to a 5.71 ERA for the first few months that year, setting the stage for a signature Philly failure moment. The scene: Phillies vs. Orioles, June 16, 2015 at Camden Yards in Baltimore. After sitting through a 4-0 Phillies loss the night before, I was hoping for something better on this occasion, and Williams was on the mound. In an all-timer, even for Phillies pitchers, Williams lasted 2/3 of an inning, giving up six runs on two walks and four hits. He also threw two wild pitches. He mercifully exited the game AFTER INJURING HIMSELF COVERING HOME PLATE ON THE SECOND WILD PITCH and the Phillies went on to lose 19-3. The 19 runs is the most I've ever seen in person. Williams' ERA rose to 6.43 on the season after that bloodbath but he was able to trim that down to a neat 5.80 by years' end after missing a month with the injury. Needless to say, he was not invited back.

30. Vincent Lecavalier – This guy used to be really good; make no mistake. But when he came to the Flyers at age 33, he already had a ton of mileage on him. His five-year, $22.5 million contract was immediately cringe-worthy and seemed to be one of those "Flyers moves" where they pick up a big slow guy and not only overpay him, but pay him based on what he had done in the past rather than potential future returns. This assessment was correct. Vinny was a bust. In 133 games over three seasons with the team, he scored just 28 goals and added 30 assists. He was shipped off to the Kings finally, playing out the rest of the 2015-16 season with them and then retiring.

29. Desi Relaford – Poor Desi. He will forever be a punchline for me and my friends because he was the perfect embodiment of how bad the Phillies were in the late 1990's. You can hide a player like Desi if your team is good and he plays a utility role, but the Phillies trotted him out there as their everyday shortstop for the better part of two seasons while he accumulated a .234 average in over 1000 AB. He did have nine dingers during his time with the team though. So, even though Desi made this list, we salute him. Someone has to be a surrogate for all of the pathetic hitters during this era of Phillies baseball. And so we say, for the only time ever...DESI RELAFORD, YOU ARE THE MAN!

28. Chad Ogea – Sometimes you're just so bad that your stench lingers and it seems like you were around for a lot longer of a time than you actually were. Exhibit A: Chad Ogea. He came to the Phillies in an offseason trade in exchange for the immortal Jerry Spradlin after the 1998 season. Ogea had pitched in four straight postseasons for the Indians and looked like a decent gamble for a Phillies team that needed rotation help (and help everywhere else). He was just 28 years old and could conceivably be a stabilizing force for years. Instead, Chad Ogea and all of his Ogea-ness happened. In 1999, he went 6-12 with a 5.63 ERA, allowing 36 home runs to place third in all of baseball in that category. And that was it. Just the one season in Philadelphia. Sure seemed way longer than that. Ogea never pitched in the majors again, as no one was ever desperate enough to give him a shot. He somehow still finished over .500 for his career though, at 37-35.

27. DeMarco Murray – Leave it up to Chip Kelly to bring in a running back that didn't fit his scheme at all right after the Cowboys had absolutely pounded him into the ground the previous year by giving him 450 touches from scrimmage. The result was perhaps the most predictable season in Eagles history as Murray stunk, feuded with the coach, complained to the owner about his usage, got benched, hurt the team, and then got traded after just one year in town. Other than that, things turned out great.

26. Wayne Gomes – Gomes had toiled in the obscurity of middle relief for three years entering the 2000 season. Early in that campaign, I went down to Atlanta to see the Phillies play (lose) a couple games against the Braves. It was then and there that Gomes earned a permanent spot on this list. I was there early enough to watch the Phillies warming up down the right field line. Gomes, wearing a windbreaker so you couldn't just identify him from the back of his jersey, was nearest to me having a catch. I recognized him and repeatedly called his name. But God forbid that he flip a ball to the only kid in the section wearing Phillies gear. Clearly I was audible because I did later get a ball from short-lived stinky starter Chris Brock. And so, from that moment, I hated Wayne Gomes. I would get my revenge on July 27, 2001 when I was on hand to see Gomes' final game as a Phillie. He was given extended mop-up duty in a road loss to the Mets at Shea Stadium, and we were questioning why they had left him in so long. Almost immediately after the game, it was announced that he had been traded to the Giants. The Wayne Train had left Philly forever. Smiles all around.

25. Glenn Robinson – The Big Dog came to the Sixers in 2003 to provide a second scoring option to Allen Iverson. Now, maybe it was just a simple fact that nobody could put up good numbers riding shotgun to "The Answer" because he needed the ball too much. Still, Robinson had averaged over 20 points per game in 8 of his 9 seasons prior to coming to Philly, but saw that drop to just 16.6 PPG in his one season for the Sixers. Not only that, but his brittle 30-year old body broke down and he missed half the season. The team also failed to make the playoffs despite the Eastern Conference being putrid that year. That was it for him in Philadelphia, as he was traded during the next season as part of one of the NBA's patented salary dump trades before ever "recovering" from whatever "injury" he had. A true dog. All this for just $10.7 million.

24. Roberto Hernandez – Take your pick. The Phillies have had two pitchers named Roberto Hernandez. The elder Hernandez was a two-time All-Star that was supposed to be the team's primary setup man for the 2004 season. But all that Roberto did was set up other teams' bats to the tune of a 4.76 ERA, his worst in a decade. The second Roberto Hernandez (nee Fausto Carmona) started 2014 with the Phillies and was half-decent before being traded to the Dodgers for some batting practice balls. Ok, he's not really deserving of being on this list, but he gets lumped in because of the Hernandez that preceded him by ten years. I can't wait until 2024 when the Phillies trot out the next one!

23. John Vanbiesbrouck – "Beezer" basically carried a talent-strapped Florida Panthers team to the Stanley Cup Final in 1996 (including a big upset over the Flyers) before ultimately running out of gas. Two seasons later, Flyers management cheaped out and opted to sign him over Curtis Joseph and proclaimed him their latest "ultimate solution in goal" that would bring that elusive Cup back to town. His first season was largely successful, but the playoffs were bizarre. Despite only giving up nine goals in six games, many of the goals he did allow were softies and should have been easily stopped. Thus, he was scapegoated for the team's first round ouster. The next year was more of the same, but he was supplanted by rookie Brian Boucher in net and watched the playoffs from the bench. During the 2000 offseason, he was traded to the Islanders and ceased to exist at that point as far as I'm concerned.

22. Todd Pinkston – Wafer-thin Todd wasn't completely without talent, but he really took the heat from the fans when the results weren't there. He made some big plays, but unfortunately those were all washed away by his lack of toughness (I wouldn't go over the middle if I was 90 pounds either) and his legendarily terrible NFC Championship Game against the Panthers when he was held without a catch, although that finally gave the Eagles the kick in the pants they needed to go out and get Terrell Owens. Was he deserving of the "Stinkston" moniker? Maybe not, if he had been put in the right role on the right team. But as a starter for this team for multiple seasons, he earned it.

21. Phillippe Aumont – You'll notice a disturbing trend of many Phillies pitchers turning up on this list. I can think of none as putrid in the post-World Series hangover years as this guy. A former first round pick by Seattle, the Phillies should have been skeptical of the Mariners' willingness to trade him just two years later. As a reliever for the Phillies, he got into 45 games over bits and pieces of three seasons with lousy results. Then they made an ill-fated attempt to convert him to a starter. When his shot finally came, he gave up six runs in four innings, walking seven hitters in the process. The team had seen enough at that point, designating him for assignment to send him back to the minors. But Aumont had the balls to refuse the assignment and became a free agent. He never made it back to the majors and retired a year later at age 27 with a career 6.80 ERA. Truly terrible.

20. Kevin Millwood – How can a guy who pitched a no-hitter for the Phillies be on this list? Because he was Kevin Millwood. Pried away from the Braves in a trade after the 2002 season, expectations were pretty large. Unfortunately, so was he. Although he was still (allegedly) in his late-20s while playing two years for the Phils, Millwood had the body of a 53-year old, which made it particularly hilarious to watch him "run" to first base when he would manage to put the ball in play as a hitter. His results on the mound were just average, no-hitter aside, and the Phillies needed a lot more from him. Considering that he pitched for five more teams over the next eight years after leaving the Phillies, it's safe to say that he had peaked with the Braves early in his career and that they knew what they were doing when they got rid of him.

19. Ilya Bryzgalov – The Flyers, perennially in search of a goaltender to lead them to the promised land, decided in the summer of 2011 that Bryzgalov was the guy, and they essentially changed the course of the franchise to bring him in because of the mammoth contract they were giving him and its impact on the salary cap. Out were Mike Richards, Jeff Carter and their salaries. And while the Flyers brought back some key pieces in return like Wayne Simmonds and Jakub Voracek in those trades, the two departed players would be key cogs in multiple Cup teams in LA, making the Bryzgalov signing hurt even more in retrospect. And did I mention that having Bryz on board meant that the Flyers shipped young goalie Sergei Bobrovsky out of town as well? All he did was become a multiple Vezina winner (best goaltender) and all-star caliber player in Columbus. Still, all of this could have been forgiven if Ilya performed up to expectations. But he stunk. In just 99 regular season games as a Flyer, he posted a .905 save % and 2.60 GAA, which are horrible in the NHL nowadays. His one postseason for the Flyers was putrid as well. After two years, the Flyers bought out his contract and will be paying him until 2027. No, that's not a typo.

18. Mike McMahon – While some players are on this list for their performance relevant to the expectations placed upon them, once in a while you just gotta make room for a guy who was simply flat-out lousy. McMahon never should have been near this list, considering he was only brought in before the 2005 Eagles season as a third-string QB for the defending NFC champs. But as it turned out, he belonged nowhere near a football field either. All it took was one McNabb injury (plus Koy Detmer being Koy Detmer) and McMahon was thrust into the middle of a disastrous season. He was 2-5 in seven starts, completing 45.4% of his passes with just five touchdowns and eight picks. If the Eagles had the option of just forfeiting the rest of their schedule, I would have preferred that over watching the McMahon-orchestrated mess that capped off that abominable campaign.

17. Mike Mamula – Continuing on the subject of lousy Mikes, Mamula has become the time-honored example of a players' draft stock soaring at the NFL scouting combine. This is why all that stuff is pointless, people. The Eagles were so wowed that they traded three draft picks to Tampa to move up to the Bucs' #7 slot and draft Mamula. Tampa then took those three picks and drafted a Hall of Famer (Warren Sapp) with one and traded the other two picks to move up and draft another Hall of Famer (Derrick Brooks). Mamula would play five years that weren't terrible, but his play was a far cry from what he was supposed to be. When you look at what could have been, this one really hurts.

16. Adam Eaton – With the Phillies seemingly on the verge of big things, they signed Eaton to join their rotation before the 2007 season. He pitched to a 10-10 record and 6.29 ERA, but despite this the Phillies were able to make the playoffs, for which he was not included on the roster. It was more of the same in 2008, as he struggled to a 4-8 mark with a 5.80 ERA before being bumped from the rotation for the newly-acquired Joe Blanton and then sent to the minors shortly thereafter. He came back up in September but wouldn't appear in another game for the Phillies. Miraculously, the Phillies won the World Series that year despite Eaton's best efforts to prevent it, setting up the most Philly sports moment ever: fans booing Eaton at the parade. It was glorious. This one goes down as an all-timer, and Eaton will live forever in infamy because of it. He also once accidentally stabbed himself in the stomach while trying to open a DVD case with a knife. You can't make this stuff up.

15. Nnamdi Asomugha – This cornerback had made three straight Pro Bowls when the Eagles snatched him away from the Raiders before the 2011 season. And so, given his history and the huge contract that the Eagles forked over, his two years in Philly rank as yet another unqualified bust. For some reason, the rest of the NFL just refused to throw passes in his direction when he was with Oakland, but they got much bolder once he came to Philadelphia and exposed his weaknesses. His age was clearly taking its toll and he was not the player the Eagles had paid for. Also factoring in his apparent lack of connection with teammates (routinely eating lunch by himself in his car) and Asomugha just never fit from the start. As usual, a player used up all his greatness somewhere else and Philadelphia got the backwash that was left.

14. Derrick Coleman – In two stints that encompassed six seasons as a 76er, Coleman gouged the team for over $40 million while averaging just 13.9 points per game in 283 career contests with the team. Perennially overweight and underachieving, Coleman's career had already peaked by the time he came to the Sixers from the Nets at age 28. At least we got rid of Shawn Bradley in that deal. After letting Coleman walk as a free agent in 1998, the team felt the need to bring him back in 2001 for some reason in what may stand as the most complicated three-team trade in sports history. Coleman holds up as another one of those players whose effort never matched his ability. Or his wallet.

13. Rod Barajas – Barajas was a respected, veteran catcher who signed with the Phillies after the 2006 season. It seemed like a great move at the time. The team had a young backstop in Carlos Ruiz, and Barajas could split time with him and serve as a mentor. The team was on the cusp of a breakthrough, and it was a smart use of money to go out and get a guy who could provide the kind of rock solid defense behind the plate that Barajas had come to be known for. The honeymoon lasted less than two months, coming to a screeching halt on May 23, 2007. That fateful night, the Phillies took a 7-3 lead into the ninth inning against the Marlins, but closer Brett Myers was struggling. Still, they were up 7-6 with two outs. Hanley Ramirez stood at second base for the Marlins when a hit to left field looked like it had a chance to tie the game. But the throw was right on the money and came in to Barajas standing right at the plate. Ramirez was out by 20 feet to end the ballgame. Except he wasn't. Barajas inexplicably remained standing up like he was trying to keep from crapping his pants, Ramirez slid harmlessly between his legs, and the game was tied. Barajas went crazy, expecting to get a courtesy "out" call at the plate. He and Charlie Manuel were both ejected. The game continued and Myers, now throwing pitches that never should have happened, got hurt and missed two months of action. The Phillies won in the tenth inning, but it almost didn't matter. Barajas would only appear in 48 games in his lone season as a Phil, as the team realized that Ruiz was the far superior option. After all was said and done, Barajas couldn't hold Chooch's jock. You have to give it to him though, he's a real stand-up guy.

12. Shawn Bradley – The Stormin' Mormon was a rail-thin 7'6" center that played one year of college basketball and then took a two-year hiatus for a church mission, so of course the 76ers used the second overall pick in the 1993 draft on him. Bradley was good for blocking shots, but that was it. The Sixers traded him just twelve games into his third season with the team, finally admitting that their little experiment was a mistake. As I mentioned before, Derrick Coleman unfortunately came the other way in the trade. To be fair, that 1993 draft ended up being pretty week. But Bradley was a gamble that had "failure" written all over him. Even the Sixers should have seen that. But, hey, he was great in *Space Jam*.

11. Andy Ashby – This guy started his career with the Phils way back in 1991. Over parts of two seasons, he went 2-8 in 18 starts but was still selected by the Rockies in the expansion draft prior to 1993. Fair enough, as the Phillies got to the World Series that year and Ashby looked like he would never be anything. But after a horrible start in Colorado, Ashby was traded to San Diego and his career took off. Following the 1999 season, he was coming off back-to-back all-star appearances and the Phillies, looking to make a splash, traded for him to be their ace heading into the ill-fated 2000 campaign. As we all know, many athletes have cracked under the pressures of playing in Philadelphia. But few, if any, have folded as quickly as Ashby did. In half a season, he posted a 4-7 record with a 5.68 ERA and also flipped off the fans after one particularly lusty round of booing upon his removal from a horrible outing. He was traded to the Braves for the immortal Bruce Chen several weeks before the 2000 trading deadline, as the team was extremely eager to wash their hands of the toxic mess that he had become.

10. Chris Webber – Already on the backside of his career when he came to the 76ers, Webber was nevertheless expected to provide a secondary scoring option after Allen Iverson. But, as was always the case with everyone the team ever brought in, he didn't fully mesh with The Answer and was a disappointment. Shocker. He battled injuries, benchings and general malaise over parts of three seasons with the 76ers before they eventually bought out his contract. I wish someone would give me $25 million not to work for them. The highlight of his time in town was probably when he and Iverson both didn't show up for Fan Appreciation Night at the end of the 2006 season. Neither was "healthy enough" to play but didn't think it was worth their time to even show their faces in the building at the final home game of the year. Another dubious Sixers move in a long line of them.

9. Luke Schenn – When the Flyers traded James van Riemsdyk to the Maple Leafs for Schenn in a straight-up deal, it seemed like just what the team needed. In addition to shoring up the team's blueline, bringing in Luke to play with his brother Brayden might also serve to elevate both of their games. Is that a thing? I don't know. But Luke was only 22 and had already been in the league for four years, so it was widely assumed that he could develop into a stud. Instead, his offensive game never progressed at all, which resulted in every defensive miscue of his being magnified. And there were many. The Flyers simply never got a return on the $3 million plus per year that they were paying him. And it didn't help matters that JVR developed into a legitimate power forward for Toronto, regularly popping home 30 goals per year. Another gem of a move by Flyers GM Paul Holmgren. It took until his fourth season with the team, but when Schenn was packaged with the similarly lousy Vinny Lecavalier in a trade with LA, it felt like a big-time "addition by subtraction" situation.

8. Freddy Garcia – The Phillies made a big move after the 2006 season when they shipped top prospect Gavin Floyd (who ended up not being that good) and another prospect Gio Gonzalez (who ended up being an eventual all-star and 20-game winner) to the White Sox for Garcia. Freddy had been one of the better pitchers in the AL for several years, and it stood to reason that he could improve even more pitching in the National League and in front of a young team poised to take the next step. But shoulder problems surfaced almost immediately, and Garcia was bad. He became one of my favorite all-time players to complain about by providing perhaps the worst return on investment ever. In just 11 starts as a Phillie, he posted one win. All this in exchange for his $10 million salary that season. In his final start for the team, he got lifted in the second inning of a game in Kansas City after surrendering six runs. His final five hitters faced went double, home run, walk, home run, walk. He was shut down for surgery to end his miserable season but managed to stick around the league as a journeyman for another couple years elsewhere. It stands as a minor miracle that the Phillies made the playoffs in 2007 when you consider that Garcia and Adam Eaton were two of their five highest-paid players.

7. Ruben Amaro Jr. – I cheated on this one. While Amaro was tolerable and under the radar as the Phillies' "backup to the backup" outfielder for a chunk of the 1990's, he makes this list almost exclusively for his work as the team's GM over a decade later. But hey, he was a player and so he becomes eligible for this list, parameters be damned. Hired by the Phillies to a front office position right after he retired as a player, he had the misfortune of learning under Ed Wade. Thankfully he was deemed not to be ready to take the reins when Wade was fired in 2005, leading to the championship-clinching decision to hire Pat Gillick as GM instead. Right after the 2008 World Series parade, people were in an agreeable mood and were ok with the news that Gillick would be stepping down and turning things over to Amaro. And for a few years, that seemed fine. The team remained the class of the National League, although they kept taking steps back every season, going from winning it all to losing in the World Series to losing in the NLCS to losing in the first round. Amaro's huge failure manifested itself in handing out exorbitant contracts to the team's declining core as well as trading away assets for veterans that didn't end up getting the job done. He neglected the farm system and ensured the cupboard was bare when it was time to move on from the players that had won the title in 2008. This narrative obviously would have ended up very differently if Roy Halladay, Cliff Lee or any of the players he brought in could have helped the team to another championship, but they didn't, and so here we are. After a 102-win season in 2011, the team's window slammed shut and they fell off a cliff, seeing their win total plummet to 81, 73, 73 and then finally 63 in 2015, during which Amaro was finally canned. It was a move that was a long time coming. Amaro hooked on with the Red Sox as their first base coach the following season in one of the weirdest job downgrades in baseball history. At a game in Baltimore in 2016, Amaro was in the outfield during batting practice and I gave him a half-serious/half-joking "Ruben, boo!" from the stands. To my surprise, he actually turned around and acknowledged me. Seeing my Phillies hat, he had the gall to say "You're welcome for those five division titles!" Honestly I was taken aback. It was a decent comeback, albeit one that he probably practices in front of a mirror to prepare for the inevitable and deserved vitriol he was going to receive. But man, this guy was going to take credit for five division titles? He was only an assistant GM for the first two, and the last three were still a direct result of the team that his predecessors (yes, partial credit to Ed Wade) had put together. Hell, I could have "general managed" those teams to a division win. I also like to think that Ruben was tacitly acknowledging to me that the Phillies should have won at least one more World Series by not mentioning that, deciding instead to bring up some measly division titles. All this considered, I think the #7 spot on this list is well-earned.

6. David Bell – Headed into the Vet's final season in 2003, the Phillies were starting to turn the corner and needed to drum up some excitement as they prepared for their new stadium to open the following year. They did just that by signing first baseman Jim Thome in a move that was universally applauded. About a month later, they were able to sneak Bell's signing in under the radar as fans were still salivating over the thought of big Jim knocking dozens of home runs out of the park that season. Truth be told, you knew exactly what Bell would give you: about 20 home runs and 60-70 RBI to go along with a .260 average. He was an adequate third baseman. He wouldn't kill your team but wasn't going to surprise you either. If you liked Todd Zeile, you were gonna love David Bell. But Bell's first year in Phillies pinstripes sucked, as he hit just .195 and missed half the year. Then the scene shifted to Citizens Bank Park and Bell was much better, swatting 18 home runs, knocking in 77 and surprising everyone (which I said he wouldn't do) with a career high .291 average. He even managed inexplicably to hit for the cycle one game. The problem, however, was the unstoppable force known as Chase Utley. It was clearly past time that Chase take over as a franchise cornerstone at second base, but he was being blocked there by Placido Polanco. Now, Polanco was a nice player, the only thing of use that the Phillies had managed to get in the Scott Rolen trade, and he deserved to still be part of the lineup. The obvious solution was to shift Polanco over to third base, where he had experience, and let Bell hit the bricks, coming off the bench when needed. But much to the chagrin of all Phillies fans, Charlie Manuel didn't do this and even kept Utley out of the starting lineup on opening day of 2005. This elicited heavy boos from the fans at Polanco's introduction as the starting second baseman, which was a shame because he deserved better than that. A rare lapse in judgment on the part of the Philly faithful. Bell followed up his career year by reverting back to Bell form in 2005 with a .248 average, 10 home runs and 61 RBI. Utley took over at second base full-time after Polanco was shipped off to Detroit, but Bell lingered at the hot corner. His reign of terror finally ended just before the 2006 trade deadline when the Phillies sent him to the Brewers for a pitcher that never ended up appearing in the major leagues and who was listed at 6'6" and 165 pounds. Seriously. Yes, there were many Phillies who were way worse than David Bell. But merely by existing, this guy delayed the arrival of Chase Utley as a full-time MLB player. The franchise would have been better off if they had never signed him in the first place. It quite likely cost the team a longer championship window and will keep Chase Utley out of the Hall of Fame because he had to wait too long before becoming a fixture in the lineup.

5. Mike Rathje – Following the lockout that wiped out what would have been the 2004-05 NHL season, the Flyers went with their tried and true "big and tough" method by signing hulking D-men Mike Rathje and Derian Hatcher to multi-year contracts. Never mind the league's push toward youth and speed, this was what they needed. Hatcher had his issues, but we will let him off with a warning here for gutting it out for three seasons and knocking Sidney Crosby's teeth out. So instead, let's just focus on Rathje, truly one of the most disastrous free agent signings in team history. He gave the Flyers just about what they expected in his first year with the team, but you could tell that the league and its marquee young players were getting too good and too fast for dinosaurs of his ilk to keep up. By the end of the regular season, he was playing three or four fewer minutes a night than he had at its beginning, and the team's first round playoff loss only served to reinforce that the Flyers had made a rather large oopsy by giving him a 5-year, $17.5 million deal. Rathje would plod through the first couple months of the ill-fated 2006-07 season, with things coming to a head in a game on November 29, 2006, a date which will live in infamy. Rathje had already been the butt of many jokes between my "Flyer friends" and me, but on this night he would seal a permanent place in our pantheon of ridicule. I was in the building that night to watch the Flyers take on the Nashville Predators. The Flyers had just tied the game in the late stages of the third period when, with about five minutes to go, Rathje committed what may stand as the worst turnover in NHL history. He whiffed on a pass mere feet in front of his own net, leaving a loose puck for Hall of Famer Paul Kariya, who fed a wide-open teammate for a tap-in goal to put the Preds up 3-2. This would of course be the final score, something that all 18,789 people in attendance knew with 100% certainty at the moment of Rathje's boner. I'm not able to determine in my research if Rathje had another shift in that game, although I'm not sure why in God's name he would have. But it did end up being his final game as a Flyer and in the NHL. Talk about going out on bottom. The guy was 32 years old at the time but played like he was 50. The company line was that chronic hip and back issues were to blame for his shortcomings. No doubt that played a part, but I'm inclined to believe that a decision was made by the front office at that point to not let the guy back on the ice even if he could overcome his physical issues. For the next couple seasons as I worked at various Flyers games, I would routinely see Rathje, still "on the team" since he had a contract, dressed in a suit jovially riding the elevator up to the press box to watch. Not a bad gig for $3.5 million a year.

4. Billy Wagner – If you simply looked at Wagner's numbers from his two seasons with the Phillies, you would think "Wow, this guy was amazing". And, for the most part, his performance on the field was. But as previously mentioned, he totally imploded when the pressure was on in 2005, costing the Phillies a playoff appearance. Add in the abrasive personality he showed off all too frequently, and the guy became a lightning rod for the disdain of fans and his teammates alike. When Phillies fans gave a sarcastic boo after he only hit 99 mph on the gun instead of triple digits, he simply didn't understand the concept and railed against them. He got his blood money ($17 million total) for his two years as a Phil, then moved on to the Mets, making him exponentially even more hateable. While there he blew out his arm and broke down in tears. Am I a horrible human being for feeling good about this? Probably, but you can't rewrite the past and I stand by my decision. Just as Hall of Fame voters inevitably take a players' character and relationship with the media into account when deciding their worthiness, Billy is a no-brainer selection to be near the top of this list. Because it's not just about the stats you put up in this town, it's how you represent the name on the front of your jersey and the fans of this city as a whole. And Wagner is tough to top as an abject failure in that department.

3. Jonathan Papelbon – I said Wagner was "tough to top", not impossible. From the moment that Ruben Amaro Jr. and the Phillies backed a dump truck full of money up Papelbon's driveway after the 2011 season, it was painfully obvious what a mistake it was. It was clear that the Phillies' run of success was nearing an end and they needed to start reloading for the future, so handing Papelbon the biggest contract for a relief pitcher in baseball history ($50 million over four years) was just about the last thing they should have done. Papelbon continued to pitch well in the save situations he did receive, but an endless string of asinine comments and lewd behavior such as grabbing his crotch as fans booed him off the field made him one of the city's most vilified athletes in recent memory. And so it was hilarious that the Phillies were able to flip him to the Nationals at the 2015 trade deadline, a completely unnecessary move on the Nationals' part that torpedoed their season after Papelbon tried to choke out Washington star Bryce Harper during a dugout altercation. The team tacked a disciplinary suspension onto another one that he already had coming, ending his season a week early and leading him to file a grievance in the offseason. Inexplicably, the Nationals stuck with him as their closer to open 2016, but after injuries and a trade for a new closer, Papelbon was released at his request. So while he was a jackass for the Phillies, at least he didn't cost them a World Series shot like he did with the Nationals. He left the Phillies as their all-time saves leader, but we all wish that record could be wiped clean. His mere presence lent a toxic air to the team and killed any chance they may have had, however small, to make one last run with the core left over from 2008. No sane person can disagree: He never should have been a Phillie.

2. Braydon Coburn – Taken eighth overall by the Atlanta Thrashers (RIP) in the incredibly loaded 2003 NHL draft, Coburn was a hot commodity at the 2007 trade deadline. He was a young player with a lot of promise, so with the Thrashers in the midst of literally the only good season they ever had in Atlanta, Coburn was their #1 trade chip. They came calling on the cellar-dwelling Flyers, who were rightly quick to ship 34-year old defenseman Alexei Zhitnik down south to acquire Coburn. The move paid immediate dividends for the orange and black, as Coburn looked good in twenty games with an awful lineup around him to finish up the season. The Flyers reloaded over the summer, and Coburn blossomed during the 2007-08 season, racking up 9 goals and 27 assists for 36 points while playing over 21 minutes a night and posting a +17 rating. He looked like a surefire star in the making. Then, in the playoffs that season, the pendulum swung in the other direction and sent him spiraling nearly to the top (or bottom?) of this list. Coburn continued to play important minutes for the first two rounds as the Flyers surprised everyone by reaching the Eastern Conference Final against the Penguins. They were heavy underdogs and needed all of their key players at maximum capacity if they hoped to pull off an upset. The Flyers lost Game 1, and then they were dealt a crippling blow early the next game when a deflected puck caught Coburn above the eye, a gruesome injury that required fifty stiches and all but killed the Flyers' chances in that game or the series. Coburn never returned that season and the Flyers lost meekly in five games. He was up and around in plenty of time for the start of the next year, but something was off. I'm not going to get into the old-school "tough guys don't wear visors" argument, but Coburn was now donning one after his injury and his play seemed affected to me, as it was noticeably more timid. He wasn't taking advantage of his large frame, and his offensive skills seemed to have lessened overnight. Honestly, I thought he had a Chris Pronger-type ceiling, a physical blueliner that could intimidate while drilling home double-digit goals per season and playing in all situations, a clear #1 defenseman. Maybe the injury stunted his growth or maybe I'm just assigning blame to one instance and ignoring other factors, but Coburn never again matched the goal, assist, point, plus/minus or power play goal totals that he had posted in his first full season as a Flyer. The numbers bear out that he was an above average defenseman that did deliver some hits and put up decent numbers, but I believe he could have been so much better. And I'm convinced that for the next half-decade, he was on the ice for every game-deciding goal against the Flyers, standing by himself while an open man slammed home the game-winner. Check the tapes, I'm sure of it. Even when the Flyers actually traded for Pronger, his presence couldn't coax Coburn into becoming the kind of defenseman that he should have been. Coburn had a way better career in Philadelphia than almost everyone else on this list, but he fell way short of the expectations that we all had for him. If he had been merely consistent, we wouldn't have thought anything of it, but he clearly peaked too early. Maybe he didn't entirely earn the "Co-Bum" nickname that my friend bestowed upon him, but life isn't fair. All Flyers fans can tell you that.

1. Scott Rolen – Well, here we are. Number one with a bullet. And if you have me write up a new list on my deathbed, Rolen will still be right here. The whole situation is a combination of factors, starting off with the fact that he arrived with the Phillies when I was eleven years old, a very impressionable age where we tend to put athletes on a pedestal. And make no mistake, I really liked Scott Rolen. The cupboard was pretty bare for the Phillies, so they were promoting him as this generation's Mike Schmidt, the face of the franchise for years to come. After a promising audition in 1996, Rolen came out and won Rookie of the Year honors the following season. Things were going nicely. He settled in as a solid bat and perennial Gold Glover, but something was festering. It should be noted that Phillies' management was inept at that point in time and didn't do much to surround Rolen with a team that could compete for the playoffs. Terry Francona also did an atrocious job of managing the situation, compounding problems even further. Rolen's balky back didn't agree with the turf at the Vet (poor baby) and his quiet, country boy persona slowly devolved into that of a bitter and sullen young man. It was no secret; he wanted out. Since apparently every Midwestern little boy dreams of playing for the Cardinals someday, they ended up being the destination, and Indiana-born Scott couldn't have been happier to get away from the mean fans in Philadelphia and the Astroturf that hurt him so much. Never mind that the Phillies were in the process of becoming contenders and had a few decent pieces in place, as well as a new stadium on the way (with real grass and dirt!) that would have alleviated the turf problem, Scott just couldn't wait any longer. He was traded in 2002 on the day after Harry Kalas was inducted into the Hall of Fame when fans were in a good mood so that they didn't burn too many effigies of him in the street. At some point after he was traded, I bought a Rolen figurine and used it as a voodoo doll of sorts, chronicling the injuries he sustained by doing things like taping gauze to its shoulder and putting a Band-Aid on its back. Rolen would unfortunately go on to win the 2006 World Series with the Cardinals and play at an all-star level when he was healthy enough to stay in the lineup. But during the 2008 season, he was traded to Toronto, where he was reunited with his beloved turf infield. I was very pleased about this development. And when the Phillies won the World Series later that year, I took the Rolen figurine and smashed it to bits on the garage floor in a cleansing ritual of sorts. The Phillies had exorcised all traces of the Rolen stink that may have still lingered. But this was not me letting bygones be bygones, and I continued to wish Rolen ill will for the rest of his career. His only playoff appearance against the Phillies came with the Reds in 2010. He went 1 for 11 in the series, committed two errors and struck out to end the final game, which was on my birthday. It doesn't get any more satisfying than that. Rolen retired after the 2012 season. Now Hall of Fame eligible, I have heard murmurs that he could be a guy that gets in eventually. Perish the thought. I will begrudgingly admit that he was a very good player, but he is not a Hall of Famer. The ONLY way I would be fine with him making the Hall is if he is made to go in with a Phillies cap on his plaque. Rolen himself would probably sooner refuse induction than to be made to do this, but the thought makes me a little giddy. After all, he did play longer in Philadelphia than in St. Louis and basically split his Gold Glove awards evenly between those two stops. Whether you think Rolen deserves top (dis)honors or not, we can all agree that there aren't many athletes in Philadelphia history that have gone from fan favorite to chump in such a detestable fashion. Again, the situation of the franchise at the time wasn't great, but Rolen did nothing to endear himself to the fans here, and his attitude about the whole thing belied his abilities on the field. He could have been one of the best Phillies in our lifetimes, but he got in his own way and fell pitifully short of what he should have accomplished here. He is unquestionably my #1. Who's yours?

*

50 MOST DISLIKED ATHLETES QUICK REFERENCE GUIDE

1. Scott Rolen, Phillies third baseman
2. Braydon Coburn, Flyers defenseman
3. Jonathan Papelbon, Phillies reliever
4. Billy Wagner, Phillies reliever
5. Mike Rathje, Flyers defenseman
6. David Bell, Phillies third baseman
7. Ruben Amaro Jr., Phillies infielder/GM
8. Freddy Garcia, Phillies starter
9. Luke Schenn, Flyers defenseman
10. Chris Webber, 76ers forward
11. Andy Ashby, Phillies starter
12. Shawn Bradley, 76ers center
13. Rod Barajas, Phillies catcher
14. Derrick Coleman, 76ers forward
15. Nnamdi Asomugha, Eagles cornerback
16. Adam Eaton, Phillies starter
17. Mike Mamula, Eagles defensive end
18. Mike McMahon, Eagles quarterback
19. Ilya Bryzgalov, Flyers goaltender
20. Kevin Millwood, Phillies starter
21. Phillippe Aumont, Phillies reliever
22. Todd Pinkston, Eagles wide receiver
23. John Vanbiesbrouck, Flyers goaltender
24. Roberto Hernandez, Phillies reliever
25. Glenn Robinson, 76ers forward
26. Wayne Gomes, Phillies reliever
27. DeMarco Murray, Eagles running back
28. Chad Ogea, Phillies starter
29. Desi Relaford, Phillies shortstop
30. Vincent Lecavalier, Flyers center
31. Jerome Williams, Phillies starter
32. Jeff Hackett, Flyers goaltender
33. LJ Smith, Eagles tight end
34. Matt Read, Flyers winger
35. Jose Mesa, Phillies reliever
36. Ulf Samuelsson, Flyers defenseman
37. Jerome McDougle, Eagles defensive end
38. Bradley Fletcher, Eagles cornerback
39. Riley Cooper, Eagles wide receiver
40. Domonic Brown, Phillies outfielder
41. Jiri Dopita, Flyers center
42. Dennis Cook, Phillies reliever
43. Billy Tibbetts, Flyers winger
44. Chris Gratton, Flyers center
45. Ricky Watters, Eagles running back
46. Freddie Mitchell, Eagles wide receiver
47. Danny Tartabull, Phillies outfielder
48. Cary Williams, Eagles cornerback
49. Omar Daal, Phillies starter
50. Ronnie Brown, Eagles running back

List Composition

21 Phillies, 13 Eagles, 12 Flyers, 4 76ers

"Most Disliked" Positions

14: Phillies Pitchers (7 starters, 7 relievers)

5: Flyers forwards

4: Phillies infielders, Flyers defensemen

3: Eagles wide receivers, cornerbacks & running backs, 76ers forwards, Flyers goaltenders

INDEX OF MEMORABLE PHILLY GAMES ATTENDED

Mar. 28, 1992, Spectrum: Duke 104, Kentucky 103, overtime

- Christian Laettner's buzzer beater sends Duke to the Final Four, en route to the national title that year. This game has been widely acknowledged as the greatest college basketball game ever played, hence its inclusion on this list even though no Philly teams were involved.

Oct. 7, 1993, Veterans Stadium: Braves 14, Phillies 3 (NLCS Game 2)

- Braves tie series at one game apiece but the Phillies still go on to win in six games.

Oct. 21, 1993, Veterans Stadium: Phillies 2, Blue Jays 0 (World Series Game 5)

- Curt Schilling shutout cuts the Blue Jays series lead to 3-2, but Toronto wins the following game to capture their second World Series in a row.

Apr. 11, 1996, Spectrum: Flyers 3, Canadiens 2

- Flyers' final regular season home game at the Spectrum.

Jul. 9, 1996, Veterans Stadium: National League 6, American League 0

- At the 67th MLB All-Star Game, Mike Piazza wins MVP honors; Ozzie Smith's final All-Star Game.

May 25, 1997, CoreStates Center: Flyers 4, Rangers 2 (Eastern Conference Final Game 5)

- Flyers advance to the Stanley Cup Final in what ended up being the last playoff game for Wayne Gretzky and Mark Messier.

May 31, 1997, CoreStates Center: Red Wings 4, Flyers 2 (Stanley Cup Final Game 1)

- Red Wings take opening game of eventual sweep.

Dec. 15, 2002, Veterans Stadium: Eagles 34, Redskins 21

- Eagles' final regular season game at Veterans Stadium.

Sep. 28, 2003, Veterans Stadium: Braves 5, Phillies 2

- Phillies' final game at Veterans Stadium.

Mar. 4, 2004, Bright House Networks Field (Clearwater, FL): Phillies 5, Yankees 1

- Opening game at Phillies' new spring training ballpark and home to their single-A affiliate.

Apr. 12, 2004, Citizens Bank Park: Reds 4, Phillies 1

- First regular season Phillies game at Citizens Bank Park.

Mar. 19, 2008, Wachovia Center: 76ers 115, Nuggets 113

- Allen Iverson returns to Philadelphia as an opposing player for the first time.

Oct. 2, 2008, Citizens Bank Park: Phillies 5, Brewers 2 (NLDS Game 2)

- Shane Victorino hits the first grand slam in Phillies postseason history. Phillies take a 2-0 series lead, then go on to win the World Series that season.

Aug. 23, 2009, Citi Field (Queens, NY): Phillies 9, Mets 7

- Eric Bruntlett turns the 15th unassisted triple play in MLB history. It is just the second time that a game ends on such a play.

Jan. 1, 2010, Fenway Park (Boston, MA): Bruins 2, Flyers 1, overtime

- Third edition of NHL's Winter Classic. Marco Sturm scores in overtime to win the game. Danny Syvret's first NHL goal is the Flyers' only marker.

May 24, 2010, Wachovia Center: Flyers 4, Canadiens 2 (Eastern Conference Final Game 5)

- Flyers advance to the Stanley Cup Final.

Jun. 2, 2010, Wachovia Center: Flyers 4, Blackhawks 3, overtime (Stanley Cup Final Game 3)

- Claude Giroux's overtime goal gives the Flyers their first Cup Final win since 1987, but Chicago goes on to win in six games.

Oct. 23, 2010, Citizens Bank Park: Giants 3, Phillies 2 (NLCS Game 6)

- Giants win series 4-2 to advance to the World Series, which they win.

Oct. 2, 2011, Citizens Bank Park: Cardinals 5, Phillies 4 (NLDS Game 2)

- Cardinals come back from a 4-0 deficit to win, tying the series 1-1. They go on to win in five games, then eventually become World Series champions that season.

Jan. 18, 2018, Wells Fargo Center: Flyers 3, Maple Leafs 2, overtime

- Eric Lindros #88 jersey retirement night

About the Author

Kevin Lagowski resides in Wilmington, DE with his wife Rachael, son Nolan and dog Lexi. He considers himself an adopted Philadelphian thanks to his education at La Salle University and the decades of supporting his team's often hopeless causes. When he's not spending time with his family and/or watching sports, he works as a technical director in the television industry. You can read all of his Philadelphia sports writings and musings on **PhillySportsComplex.com** or check out small doses of his commentary and humor by following **@BigLagowski** on Twitter.